the
NATURAL
COZY
COTTAGE

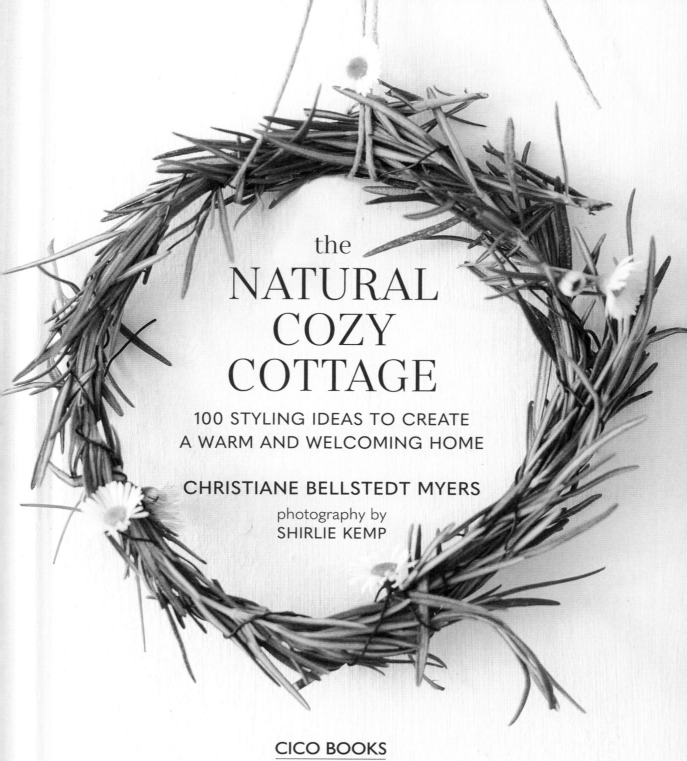

the
NATURAL
COZY
COTTAGE

100 STYLING IDEAS TO CREATE
A WARM AND WELCOMING HOME

CHRISTIANE BELLSTEDT MYERS

photography by
SHIRLIE KEMP

CICO BOOKS
LONDON NEW YORK

DEDICATION

To my parents, Brigitte and Arnulf,
who instilled the essence of cozy while
I was growing up in rural Canada.

To three charming, kind and supportive men:
my husband Neil and my sons Nicholas and
Stefan. You embraced my love of coziness
with understanding and without question.

To my daughter-in-law Meaghan and my
granddaughter Cecily, who have brought
cozy and all that it means to another level.
You have no idea how much I love you all. ♡

Published in 2022 by CICO Books
An imprint of Ryland Peters & Small Ltd

20–21 Jockey's Fields
London WC1R 4BW

341 E 116th St
New York, NY 10029

www.rylandpeters.com

10 9 8 7 6 5 4 3 2

A CIP catalog record for this book is
available from the Library of Congress
and the British Library.

ISBN: 978-1-80065-097-8

Printed in China

Editor: Sophie Devlin
Designer: Toni Kay
Photographer: Shirlie Kemp

Art director: Sally Powell
Head of production:
    Patricia Harrington
Publishing manager: Penny Craig
Publisher: Cindy Richards

MIX
Paper from
responsible sources
FSC® C106563
www.fsc.org

CONTENTS

FOREWORD

If the meaning of coziness is a feeling of "comfort, warmth and relaxation", then I know of no better person than Christiane Bellstedt Myers to write on the subject. I have known Chris, initially as a customer and then as a friend and fellow maker, for over 20 years. One cold, wet November night, I delivered a dolls' house to her home in Buckinghamshire. The front garden was open and welcoming, with lanterns lighting the path from the picket fence to the front door. I was tired after a long week at the Country Living Fair in London, and my husband and I were about to move house. In truth, I felt a bit adrift. As Chris welcomed me in, with her customary warmth, I immediately felt better. Anyone who has been to Chris's Cozy Club will recognise this feeling; it is like a comforting embrace.

In the ballad poem *The Shooting of Dan McGrew*, by Robert W Service, piano music played in a bar elicits thoughts of longing for

"... a home and all that it means;
For a fireside far from the cares that are, four walls and a roof above;
But oh! So cramful of cozy joy, and crowned with a woman's love"

Chris's home is the very essence of all that we understand as cozy. It is warm, welcoming, comfortable, pretty and, above all, personal. It is loved and cherished, and everything in it has a story. As her book demonstrates, there are many things one can do to make somewhere feel more cozy – pillows, candles, flowers, the smell of baking. However, coziness also comes from the soul of the house, and the soul of this house is Chris herself, from whom creative ideas and cozy joy emanate as naturally as an outward breath. We are fortunate indeed that she is able to share with us some of her ideas in this lovely, heartwarming book.

Caroline Zoob
July 2021

INTRODUCTION

For as long as I can remember, I have made cozy spaces within my home. It is a word that embodies all that I love: comfort, security, contentment, nature, family, friends. Nothing makes me happier than spending time in my home and making it feel like a nurturing space for people to sit for a spell. That is not saying that my home must be clinically clean and tidy at all times – far from it. Opening the door to unexpected visitors may feel overwhelming to some, but for me it is like a present. It is a chance to take a break and capture the moment. Time is precious, as we all know, and it is not to be wasted. If your home exudes the coziness that I am talking about then anyone who enters will feel welcome, calm and contented along with you. Light a candle, make some tea and relax.

When I was growing up in rural Canada, my parents instilled in me the importance of being content within our home. We always had dinner together, either in the kitchen or outside if the weather was nice. Candles were always present and it really did make each meal special. I remember on the weekends I really enjoyed our breaks together. Tea was always served at 11am and then again at 4pm. Before I moved to England to get married, the last job my father and I did was build a deck in the back garden together. The joy and satisfaction of working together to create this special space will be forever etched in my memory. This encompasses the word cozy to me.

Moving to England and having to create a home away from my family and childhood friends seemed incredibly daunting. Having a husband who allowed me to establish a home to my heart's content made all the difference. He quickly learned about the word "cozy" and let me get on with it. Together we made new traditions but the overriding feeling of coziness within our home and all that we did remained. Becoming parents and then grandparents has added so much joy to our lives and I can see that the cycle of love and coziness will continue to the next generation.

Even as a little girl, I only liked things made from wood and anything handmade was cherished. My father was a skilled carpenter and could make whatever he put his mind to. When I think back, my mother has always been the ultimate recycler. She cooks from scratch, even now at the age of 90. She recycles and brought her own bags to the grocery store before it became widespread. She hangs out her laundry in the fresh air and tends to her garden and the wildlife that visits her with love. It is not that she is doing anything out of the ordinary. She was taught not to waste and to look after nature. These principles were instilled in me from an early age. She is truly an inspiration to me.

I have always tried to live alongside nature. My meals are based on the seasons and I endeavor to buy locally. I always gather flowers, both wild and homegrown, to decorate. With all the pressures of everyday life that befall us, it is important to try to carve out time to create a simple and contented way of living. Creating a home that is naturally cozy is achievable whether you live in an old farmhouse or a city apartment. I hope, as you read this book, that I will be able to inspire you to create your own unique cozy natural home that suits you and makes you happy. After all, isn't that what life is all about? If you are contented within yourself, you will radiate that to others.

I also want to impress upon you a saying that my dear Aunt Evon once told me: "It never gets better than this." What she meant is not to wait until you think you have the perfect time to create something you would like. Do it now – perhaps it will not be exactly as you had first envisioned, but at least you will have made a start, and you can always add to it later. Life is full of unexpected occurrences; you never know what tomorrow will bring. If you make the space you are in right now as cozy and inviting as you can, you will set in motion the life you want to live.

CREATING A COZY HOME: The Elements

A pitcher full of roses or heavily scented lilacs, the fragrance of woodsmoke and damp leaves, and a piece of glass worn smooth by the waves: all these objects bring delight and connect us to the natural world. We are slowly realizing that life's simple pleasures are more fulfilling than accruing vast amounts of possessions. The earth has limited resources, and we must use what is on offer with respect and dignity.

Creating a natural cozy cottage begins when you start working alongside nature. I throw open windows and doors to let in the fresh air at all times of the year. Imagine the scent of freshly cut grass in the spring and summer or the evocative tang of a wood fire on a cold winter's day. Natural light, too, is instantly uplifting, creating a cheerful ambiance that artificial light cannot compete with. If a room is dark, reconsider the wall colors and window treatments. Mirrors can also make a room feel brighter by reflecting the available light.

Choosing colors for your rooms can be difficult. I stick to neutral hues, adding stronger color in the shape of textiles and furniture. As a result, my rooms flow seamlessly from one to the other, creating a calm and serene feel. Having neutral shades on the walls and floors allows me to transform a room by adding different colors to match the changing seasons.

Texture is another element that gives a home its own personality. The use of cotton, wool and linen along with wood, glass and found objects is so important. Perfect condition is not a prerequisite. Weather-worn stones, a fallen branch or a mended quilt add comfort and interest. Such objects entice one to touch and feel, encouraging us to experience the environment we have created with all our senses.

The words disposable and discard are being replaced by repurpose, recycle and reclaim. It is heartwarming to see items from a bygone era being used time and time again. Finding furniture that had a life before you owned it adds history to your space. Clues such as an initial carved into the base of an old chair or a date pencilled underneath a table ignite the imagination. When these objects join your home, their new chapter begins with you.

Now more than ever, outdoor space is highly valued. Our gardens have become extensions of our living rooms, somewhere we can play, gather and grow. Firepits enable us to lengthen the time we can stay outside no matter the time of the year. There is a renewed appreciation of nature – gathering pinecones to make a wreath or finding the first sprig of greenery after a long winter makes everyday life special.

A natural cozy home is filled with objects of necessity, and each should have a practical use as well as being lovely to look at and use. Take time to assess all that you own. No doubt, you will place many things in the donation box. Not only are you clearing your home of clutter, but your generosity will make someone else happy. Living simply and being guided by nature is more enriching than anything you can buy.

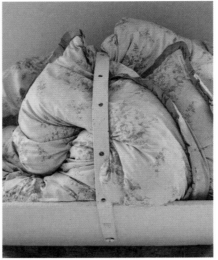

Textiles

Including a variety of textiles is an easy way to give your home a lived-in look. The odd patch or frayed hem only brings character to the spaces you love. Thick curtains will keep winter drafts at bay, while carefree voile or muslin panels let in fresh summer breezes.

An abundance of pillows placed randomly around a room will always encourage people to sit and relax. Pillows are a wonderful decorating tool, as they are simple and inexpensive to change with the seasons. My mother made our family a mountain of little pillows out of my father's old shirts, fashioned so that each one had an original shirt pocket in the front. In every pocket, she placed a sweet little note that the recipient would appreciate. What lovely mementos they were, and very special for each person.

Rugs are a great way to enhance your home during the colder months, and simple handmade braided rugs are ideal for this. Next to your bedside, consider placing a soft mat to welcome your first stretch of the morning.

I love the look of quilts in every corner of my home. I enjoy the fact that they are made from saved scraps that were sewn together to make a new, useful and decorative heirloom. Little did the women who created these quilts know that their handiwork would still be so cherished centuries later. As I wrap a quilt around my shoulders, I think about its maker and imagine what she must have been like. A lot of love went into the creation of these quilts, which makes them priceless to me. All these textiles encourage us to linger longer.

ABOVE FROM LEFT *Mixing patterns is almost a rule for a charming country cottage look – just make sure that the colors complement one another and the patterns will sit side by side quite happily. A well-loved eiderdown is ready to be snuggled into at a moment's notice. This muted scheme includes a pillow made from an old grain sack.*

OPPOSITE *Roses never fail to please. The curtain in the cupboard echoes the just-harvested blooms, while homespun pillows mingle happily with the eiderdown and painted pitcher. The gingham heart is one of many throughout my home.*

Lighting

Choosing the right kind of light for your home can be confusing. Overhead lights, dimmer switches, individual lamps, spotlights... the list goes on. But the first thing I think of when I look at a room is where I can safely place candles – morning, noon and night.

OPPOSITE *My dining room looks lovely bathed in only candlelight. I have but one small lamp, which is covered with a gingham shade. It is normally only used when the room is unoccupied, as it shines so sweetly to the outside. I love it when a home looks warm and inviting to passers-by.*

ABOVE FROM LEFT *An old chandelier gives my bathroom a rustic charm. A 100-year-old spindle with its original paint has been transformed into a pair of candleholders (see page 84). Foliage and flowers decorate the chandelier in my dining room.*

Imagine an empty room. Now imagine the same room with a candle. Instantly the space becomes cozy and you are drawn to the flame and its soft glow.

In rooms where a lot of work must be done on a daily basis, I suggest spotlights within the ceiling. They are unobtrusive and provide the appropriate amount of light. In areas where you are seeking comfort and relaxation, table and floor lamps are preferable and these can be easily changed around when redecorating. Lamps that bend or swivel are ideal beside the reading chair, while candles add atmosphere. My dining room has no artificial light – candlelight provides all the light that we need and

encourages friends and family to chat long after the meal has finished.

Natural light is, of course, the best, so keep window treatments to the minimum if your windows are small. Where light is scarce, consider transom windows. These windows above a door allow natural light to reach darker spaces. Mirrors and light-colored paint will make a room feel lighter as well. Before decorating, look at how the light moves around the space. Observing it at different times of the day will help you choose the right palette. Finally, decorate so that your heart sings every time you walk into your home. After all, isn't that what you are trying to achieve?

Furniture

Furniture can be tricky. Many of us have at least one inherited piece that we feel we cannot get rid of. My question is, do you love it? If not, look at it again. Can it be painted or altered? Do you even like it? Remember that your home has to make you happy.

I have been finding wonderful items in dumpsters/skips, yard/car-boot sales and second-hand stores for years. Every object in my home has a story attached to it, from the smallest framed picture in my living room to the sweet iron beds in the nursery. Finding a piece when you are not actually looking for it is a most serendipitous occurrence. Getting it home, cleaning it up and finding a spot where it will live is an adventure that I will never grow tired of.

Keep in mind that a piece made or designed for a certain area may also work elsewhere. I have an antique French wrought-iron daybed, originally made for a nursery, which is now happily residing under my stairs. Large items, such as a sofa or a gorgeous old farmhouse table, can weather many years and, with love and care, will last beyond your lifetime. An old apple crate can be used as a bookshelf or bedside table. A blanket chest makes an ideal coffee table, while an old door could be used as a headboard. I found a rusty old chandelier in my Aunt Evon's garden. She had no use for it, so it ended up hanging in my bathroom. I had no intention of getting a chandelier, but it is now obvious that I needed one. Imagination and the will to get your hands dirty are all that is needed to create an individual, interesting and cozy home.

ABOVE FROM LEFT *It is very simple to change the feeling of my porch by switching the textiles and blooms that decorate this old bench. Similarly, adding fresh flowers to any room in your home will highlight the time of year. Using pieces of furniture outside their usual setting, as demonstrated by this bistro chair in my bathroom, adds interest.*

OPPOSITE *A nook in my hallway would never have seemed the right spot for this old French iron bed, but it is the perfect place to sit and put on your shoes. The baskets underneath hold all our mittens and hats.*

Cozy Collections

What constitutes a collection? To me, it means a set of objects that evoke memories and joy. In my reading room I have two pairs of slippers that were once worn by my boys. When I look at them, I am reminded of the day I bought them in London with my friends Geraldine and Laila 30 years ago.

OPPOSITE *My assortment of blue-and-white china will never stop growing. I know that every piece has been well loved, as the patterns are faded in places and there is the odd chip. Their history makes this gathering of cups and saucers even more interesting.*

ABOVE FROM LEFT *My sweetest and smallest collection comprises these slippers worn by my boys. Fabric hearts are by far my biggest collection and each has a heartwarming story to tell. A few of my* Anne of Green Gables *books have inscriptions that show they were given with love.*

I think of that carefree day with the dearest of friends and I remember my boys, now young men. This little vignette is so much more than the word "collection" implies. It is the key to a memory of a special time in my life.

My collection of old *Anne of Green Gables* books has become very precious to me. I first read these stories as a young girl and they evoke a simple, rural Canadian life. I often place cherished cards and notes within the pages where they flutter out when I reread the books.

Old samplers stitched by little girls years ago also represent a different way of life. Each tells a story through pictures, letters and numbers. These stitcheries were part of the girls' education to enable them to read, sew and become competent housewives. I collect samplers that are rough and simple, suggesting that they were wrought by less privileged children. Every time I gaze upon them, I have an overwhelming desire to give the little creator a big hug. What kind of life did she have all those years ago?

These are but a few of my cozy collections. They give me such pleasure and when I am out antiquing it is always exciting to find more to add to them. Be guided by what you love. Fitting it into your home will be easy because it is an extension of your cozy style.

PART 1

THE COZY ROOMS

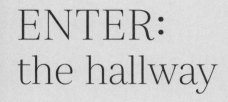

CHAPTER 1

ENTER:
the hallway

Knocking on a front door adorned with a beautiful homemade wreath makes one feel welcome before the door is even opened. Add to that a bucket of fresh flowers by the doormat and you could not ask for a warmer reception. Always make sure that your entrance is looking fresh and clean – a coat of paint can work wonders. The hallway, too, needs to make an impression on those who enter. Whether small or large, it should be free of clutter and provide an area to hang up outerwear. A well-placed mirror can make the space feel bigger, and a pitcher of flowers is always a joy to see.

I am fortunate to have a hallway that is big enough to have a row of hooks upon a wall for coats and hats. However, every wall has a door leading to another room, so there is little space for furniture. My coat area is simply a piece of wood with hooks attached. Here we hang hats and bags, coats and cardigans. From time to time, I do need to go through what is hanging there, as it is always a tempting place to leave sweaters and scarves among other items. Try to keep only seasonal clothing in this area to minimize clutter.

The wooden staircase, which used to be carpeted, is now painted warm white to match the floors elsewhere in the cottage. I have decorated the uppermost risers with wallpaper offcuts (see page 31). Under the staircase

RIGHT *My staircase has a starring role in my hallway. It is in perfect shape except for a small hole at the bottom, for which I asked my husband to make a door. In due course, this little mouse moved in. Dressed in a red coat, she sits quietly and watches the world go by. You must be very observant to even see her. A little whimsy adds so much love and personality to a home.*

is a little area that we could have boxed in to create more storage. However, I like the architectural look of the staircase, so I chose to leave it open. Over the years, I have experimented with different pieces of furniture to enhance this space, from small cupboards to little tables. I love moving furniture about, and the hallway is no exception. My favorite piece here is a French iron bedstead that we found at a sweet little antique shop in Derbyshire not long ago. It had been dismantled and was leaning against a brick wall on the outside of the building, where it had been left undisturbed for so long that it was covered in a flowering creeper. Checking first to see if it was for sale, and mindful of its age, we gently prised it from the wall and put it together. It was darling, so we quickly bought it and bundled it into the car without further ado. The problem was that I really had no idea where it would go. But then, I always worry about that sort of thing later.

Once home, I scrubbed and oiled the iron frame, while imagining how the bed might look in various spots. I finally decided to try it in the hallway, and there it found its home. It sits nestled under the stairs, complete with a simple old linen sheet, an eiderdown and some pillows. Who would have thought that a bed in a hallway would look so perfect? This is exactly what I love. No one can say what does and does not look right in a space. It has to be decorated with what you love and what makes you happy. I am already imagining this area decorated for Christmas, with a little tree adorned only with white lights beside the iron bed heaped with red and white quilts. As friends and family enter on a dark stormy night, they will be greeted by a scene of warmth and coziness.

ABOVE *This old metal daybed fits perfectly under the stairs. It makes this little space both pretty and functional, and the baskets underneath house mittens and hats. Seasonal decorating is an easy and enjoyable task, as I can simply change the soft coverings. The little stool is a lovely place for flowers.*

THE WARREN

HANG UP YOUR HAT I love using old hooks in all rooms and the hallway is the perfect spot. I prefer attaching the hooks to a board rather than directly to the wall. The reason for this is that the hooks receive a lot of wear and tear and could eventually be pulled out of the wall, leaving a messy hole. A wooden board is a strong alternative and looks great. As the hallway is usually quite a small space, it is a good idea to paint the board the same colour as the wall.

SPECIAL DELIVERY In small confined areas, the need for a designated spot for various items is ideal. If you have a letterbox in your front door, letters invariably fall onto the floor. Outside our front door is a simple box, painted the same colour as the door, with the word POST stencilled on it. The box is big enough to hold most letters, magazines and small parcels. It keeps them dry and the hallway stays warm because the letterbox in the door is covered (see page 31).

READY AND WAITING In order to decorate my front door quickly and easily, I have attached small nails all the way round the door frame about 30cm apart. I have painted the nails white so that they blend into the paintwork. They allow me to attach greenery and twinkle lights with ease. Occasionally, I will put up some wire all the way round and then attach fresh flowers, little jars and bottles or anything else that strikes my fancy. It is an easy way to make sure I am always ready when the urge to decorate strikes.

BEAUTIFUL BLOOMS

Fresh flowers from the garden look delightful when arranged in a bucket or pitcher on the front step of your home. The added benefit of leaving the flowers outside is that they last that much longer. Cut daffodils, for instance, will last for over a month outside. It is quite amazing. In the autumn, place a bucket full of branches, with the leaves beginning to show their colors, on your doorstep instead.

RING THE BELL Door knockers are often not heard unless you are close by. I have solved this problem by hanging up an ancient bell on a rope next to my front door. The pleasing sound announces guests in a loud but very friendly way.

GUIDING LIGHT Having a little lantern hanging safely by your front door is a most welcoming sight. The warm glow instantly triggers a feeling of calm. Years ago, I started lighting a lantern at about 5pm to welcome my husband home from work during the winter months. When I am in the front garden, often strangers will stop to remark how much they have enjoyed this small beacon of warmth as they passed by on their way home from the train station. Of course, hearing this made me very happy, and it confirmed my belief that little things matter – an outside lantern, a little jar of fresh flowers beside the bed or a heap of old magazines left on a doorstep for someone you know will love them. These thoughtful gestures cost nothing but bring incomparable joy to others. This is the essence of being cozy.

"Fresh flowers from the garden look delightful when arranged in a bucket on the front step of your home."

Make ideas

Friendship Staircase

Not long ago, a dear friend in Norway, Geraldine, began wallpapering her living and dining rooms. The papers she was using were a soft Swedish gray with a very subtle pattern. I thought they were so beautiful and then remembered that another friend, Sophie, had used wallpaper to decorate her staircase risers. Geraldine loved the idea, and several remnants of her wallpaper landed on my doorstep in no time. My "friendship staircase" at the top of the house reminds me of wonderful times we have spent together. I wrote the story of the wallpaper's provenance on the risers before I glued the paper on to create a sort of time capsule. I think finding history beneath wallpaper and hidden under stairs and in fireplaces so lovely, it is certainly worth doing in your own home.

MATERIALS
ruler · paper scissors · wallpaper remnants · PVA glue · damp sponge

1 Measure the risers of your staircase and cut the wallpaper to the right size. If you only have several smaller pieces, put them together and try to match up the pattern as best you can.

2 Apply the glue to the risers, then affix the wallpaper.

3 Use a damp sponge to smooth out the wallpaper and leave to dry.

Letterbox Flap

If you have a letterbox in your front door and do not want to replace it with a box outside the door, I suggest that you simply take a rectangular piece of wood, slightly larger than the size of the slot, and add two hinges to attach it to the inside of the door. Mine has a heart cut out in the wood and is backed by gingham fabric. This flap allows letters to enter but keeps the cold air out. It also adds charm to the space.

MATERIALS
ruler · wooden plank · 2 small hinges · screws and screwdriver · fabric or other materials of your choice, for decoration

1 Measure your slot and add ½in/1cm on each side to determine the length and width required.

2 Cut the wood to the right size and attach the hinges using screws.

3 Decorate the wooden flap as you wish.

4 Use more screws to attach the hinges to the inside of the door so that the flap covers the slot of the letterbox.

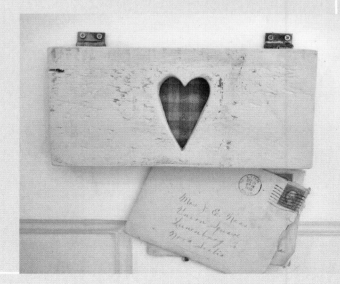

GATHER:
the kitchen

The kitchen is a space that is invariably filled with many memories, as it is the room where most people tend to congregate. It is usually the place where we begin and end our day. My kitchen is filled with modern conveniences but at the same time conjures up images of days gone by. Dishwashing is made easy by having the dish soap and towels close at hand. Pretty mugs hanging on a shelf accompanied by jars of fresh flowers bring a kitchen to life – the joy of seeing these little posies alongside items for daily use is both comforting and beautiful.

OPPOSITE *My Aga range cooker greets me each day with the warmest of hugs. As I tiptoe downstairs early in the morning I have but one thing on my mind and that is to snuggle close to this hunk of iron and make a cup of tea. It is indeed a luxury, but I excuse the expense as it will last a lifetime.*

ABOVE *Old tins are an inexpensive and eco-friendly way to keep food fresh. Simply place a piece of parchment paper over the contents, making sure there is an overhang, before you close the lid.*

RIGHT *My butler's sink has served me well. It is deep enough to clean the biggest of pans and to fill up tall pitchers of water for flowers. Open shelves for plates and bowls make tidying up a joy rather than a chore. I collect dishes with different patterns in similar colors for a cohesive look.*

Freestanding cupboards, open shelving and glass-fronted hutches/dressers all display items to be used on a daily basis. Nests of bowls, plate racks filled with mismatched crockery and rows of mason jars and vases display their beauty and utility. Natural materials are certainly prevalent in this room: wooden tables serving as work stations, wicker baskets and terracotta floor tiles. The large sink is both pleasing and practical. I like to get up very early in the morning and usually drink my first cup of tea sitting in this room.

No matter how small my kitchens have been in the past, I have always made room for a comfortable chair, fresh flowers and a basket of tealights. I had a sweet little kitchen when we were first married and it did not take me long to dismantle the fitted cabinets, paint the remaining cupboards a cheerful powder blue and install a reclaimed butler's sink to replace one made of plastic.

A simple kitchen equipped with all the essentials does away with the need for large amounts of storage space. Add a pitcher of flowers and a few homemade cleansers and you will soon have a natural cozy kitchen.

TOP ROW *A collection of mismatched blue-and-white plates. This old Canadian tea caddy was a wonderful find in Nova Scotia – once I read the wording, I knew it had to come home with me. A posy of flowers will add a special cottage charm.*

BOTTOM ROW *I started collecting old, well-loved fabric hearts when I was 12. This one adorns my basket*

of antique cookie cutters. Vintage preserving jars are perfect for keeping utensils neat and tidy. Baking soda is a great natural cleanser, so I keep a jar of it next to the sink with a handy scoop.

OPPOSITE *The painted shelves above the sink are antique – however, my husband added the top shelf, which allows for more storage.*

LEFT *This tall table was once much shorter. My husband simply added another layer of planks to make it a more comfortable work surface. He also added the two antique storage boxes underneath. The little French shelving unit beside the Aga was found at the Decorative Living Fair at Eridge Park in Sussex. I attached the old-fashioned glass drawers to the bottom, which are so helpful when I am cooking.*

ABOVE *This old farmhouse table could tell many delightful stories. The position of the table allows friends and family to have a gorgeous view of the garden. The table has many uses, from desk (where I am writing this now) to dining area and kitchen worktop. It beckons all to come and stay for a spell – the chairs have inviting cushions and the chandelier offers a cozy atmosphere when dining.*

Kitchen style ideas

PRESERVING THE PAST Glass mason jars, used to preserve food during the meager months, were a necessity for kitchens in days gone by. These vessels made sure that winter would not be quite so bleak for their former owners. Glass jars with lids work equally well. I am always so happy when I come across an old jar to add to my collection – they are easily attainable at fairs or second-hand shops. I have arranged mine in rows on the hutch/dresser in my kitchen, leaving room for a small tealight or ornament here and there. The jars hold all my dry goods and make it easy to see if I need to replenish anything. The different hues of the jars hint at their ages and add warmth to the display. I paste labels onto the bottom of each jar as a helpful and unseen reminder of what each one contains.

HEART AND SOUL

I have many wooden boards scattered about ready to be used. They look more and more beautiful the older they become. I have a number of smaller heart-shaped boards that I use for breakfast or snacks. They are great for a quick clean-up as well, as I can simply wipe them with warm water. From time to time I scrub them with a mixture of coarse salt and lemon juice, which cleans the board and acts as a natural sanitizer.

FROM TRUG TO TABLE Flatware/cutlery and kitchen utensils are essential items, but having drawers full of duplicates is not a necessity. I suggest you go through your utensils regularly – take out those you do not use and donate them so that they can find a new home.

Placing my knives, spoons and forks in separate jars in a wooden trug makes setting the table a quick chore and putting clean items away very easy. I keep them on the table near the dishwasher. One side of the trug holds the flatware, the other fabric napkins for the week.

BRING THE OUTSIDE IN I have many open shelves in my kitchen and I like to change the feel of them from time to time. I love to invite nature into my home and will go out daily to see what is blooming. To enhance the shelves, I gather a little bundle of greenery or the odd bloom and place them here and there. At the moment, I have little jars filled to the brim with lilacs – the scent is gorgeous. It takes but a few minutes and not only does it look pretty, it gives you a chance to walk outside and really see what is growing. If you do not have a garden, do not let that stop you. Head outdoors for a stroll and see what is around. Perhaps there is an open area where you are allowed to gather some of nature's beauty and bring it home to decorate your space. If that fails, then I suggest you head to your local grocery store and purchase some herbs in little pots. These look so sweet tucked into an old wooden box on a window ledge. They will both be beautiful to look at and also lovely to use while cooking.

LIGHT A CANDLE I cannot live without candles glowing at some point during the day in spring, summer, autumn and winter. One of the first things I do when I get up in the morning is come downstairs into the kitchen and light some tealights. These little candles are a very inexpensive way to cozy up any room in your home and they look so sweet positioned in safe places all around the kitchen. They are just perfect, as the flame only lasts a couple of hours. I like to place single tealights into old French bakery molds. These containers are the ideal size and serve to protect the furniture from the hot candle. You can find molds with a lovely patina at fairs and antique shops. I have an assortment of different sizes and they look amazing grouped together or on their own. I usually arrange them in odd numbers; this is my rule of thumb in most displays.

A CORNER TRANSFORMED
An awkward corner in a kitchen needs just a little imagination to turn it into something special. If you have such a space anywhere in your home, simply add an old ladder. If the rungs are no longer safe, it might otherwise be destined for the scrapheap, but these can be simply changed to hold some seasonal decoration. Each rung can hold a lantern, a small bucket of flowers, dish towels… the possibilities are endless. Simply clean the ladder and paint it if needed. Lean it in a corner against the wall and have fun decorating – it is as simple as that.

SOMEWHERE TO SIT If you feel that your kitchen is too small for a cozy chair, look again. You could exchange a plain chair for one that is more comfortable to sit upon. A small bench with a soft cushion is better than nothing and it makes the area so much more inviting and comforting to look at. It is lovely for visitors to linger and relax in comfort with you.

PRETTY AND PRACTICAL I grew up using cloth napkins at every meal. I did not realize it then, but this concept is both eco-friendly and useful. It is lovely to use different seasonal fabrics for the napkins and a great way to use up any fabric scraps you may have. All you need to do is hem a square piece of fabric on all sides.

A PLACE FOR EVERYTHING If you are anything like me, you find it difficult to throw anything away that could perhaps be useful one day. This is a good idea, but the way to steer clear of clutter is to make sure you have a place for all the remnants you are saving. In particular, I like to keep each fragment of ribbon and string, no matter how small. They are kept neatly in jars that are dotted about in my kitchen, sewing area and boot room. I often head to these jars when I need just a short piece of string for tying up a plant or a ribbon to wrap around a little present. It really is amazing how useful they become.

> "I like to keep each fragment of ribbon and string, no matter how small."

WASTE NOT, WANT NOT Old storage tins hark back to past times, when waste was all but non-existent. I so enjoy collecting these objects, each one telling its own story. My favorite is a collection of tins that someone with imagination made to look like a set. She painted five ordinary tins the same shade of green and then carefully painted on what the tin contained. To my utter amazement, one tin was marked "crumbs". This is exactly what we should all aspire to and we need to instill such a mindset in today's throwaway society.

SEW STYLISH I wear aprons all the time. They are useful and I think very pretty. I will often make one out of an old dish towel that I find particularly sweet. If you do this, there is practically no sewing required – you just need to attach some ribbons on each side. There are some lovely old French examples to be found that are extra long and make superb aprons. If I am visiting someone who shares my love of stylish aprons, I will make one and use it as wrapping, perhaps for a bottle of homemade cordial. This never fails to please.

CUTTERS WITH CHARACTER I love to bake. Growing up
I was the one who was in charge of baking the birthday cakes,
and I started collecting cookie cutters before I was married.
These inexpensive small shapes, especially older ones, have so
much character and are so pleasing to use. Some even have little
handles attached to them. Cookies that are made using them
elicit smiles from one and all. Every time I find an old cutter at a
fair I feel it has to come home with me. My collection is housed in
an old basket under my sink. They have been used as stencils for
little ones to draw around and I have also used them for making
wreaths. At Christmas they are hung on the tree in my kitchen.
I go through my collection regularly and if I find I have duplicates,
they will appear tied with string to a present for someone special.

Make ideas

Quilt Window Curtain

Quilts are without a doubt one of my favorite things. One can never have too many. It does not matter if they are threadbare; in fact, that makes me love them all the more. These charming covers, made with the fabric of old clothing, tell such an important story of "make do and mend". I marvel at the makers and always, when a quilt is wrapped around my shoulders, I give thanks to the person who created it and I imagine to whom it might have belonged. I like to use quilts in all my rooms and have made a few into curtains. It was very hard at first to cut up a quilt that was so lovingly made, but I eventually found the courage to do so and I do think the maker would approve. My winter curtains are thick and mostly red whereas my spring and summer ones are light in color and weight. They each get a thorough cleaning before they are folded away to be brought out again at the appropriate time.

MATERIALS
an old quilt • curtain wire • 2 pairs of hooks and eyes

1 Measure the window you wish to cover.

2 Cut the quilt to fit the window but try to snip it as little as possible and leave it intact if you can. It does not matter if the finished curtain is slightly too long.

3 Fold over the top of the fabric and sew a pocket for the curtain wire.

4 Cut the curtain wire to the right length.

5 Attach the hooks to the window frame and the eyes to the ends of the wire. Pass the wire through the pocket of the curtain.

6 Hang the quilt curtain for a cozy window treatment.

Dishwasher Curtain

Modern conveniences are a necessary part of our lives, but many of us prefer not to look at them. A simple way of disguising a dishwasher is to make a curtain for it. The fabric must be robust enough to withstand daily use. I have found that the best by far comes from old grain sacks, which I find at antique fairs. Any stains or mends just add character and each has a story to tell.

MATERIALS
fabric of your choice • curtain wire • 2 pairs of hooks and eyes

1 Select your fabric and measure the width and height of the dishwasher.

2 Cut the fabric so that the width is one and a half times the width of the dishwasher. Hem the length to slightly longer than the height of the dishwasher.

3 Fold over the top of the fabric to the right length and sew across to make a pocket for the curtain wire to pass through.

4 Cut the curtain wire to the right length.

5 Attach the hooks to the dishwasher enclosure and the eyes to the ends of the curtain wire. Pass the wire through the pocket of the curtain.

6 Hang the curtain – the fabric should have a gathered appearance.

Selbst in der kleinsten A

In bester Ordnung se

Directions
for Making
Melrose's Tea

lways use fresh water
warm a suitable sized
teapot and put in the dry Tea
be sure the water is thoroughly
and unmistakably boiling while
being poured on the tea.
It is thus better to bring
teapot to the kettle
kettle to the teapot
till the teapot to the
keep it warm und
added tea-cosie
how the tea to
10 to 15 min
d sugar and cr

granulated
Sugar

Palmers Biscuits

CADBURY'S
COCOA ESSENCE

ABSOLUTELY PURE   NO CHEMICALS USED.
No 7.   1/6 TINS   1 Doz

STORAGE COMPANY
PEPPER
VINTAGE STYLE
ESTABLISHED 1888

CHAPTER 3

STORE:
the pantry

During my childhood, my favorite books were classics such as *Anne of Green Gables*, *The Secret Garden*, *The Railway Children* and *Little Women*. It was terribly exciting for me when these books made it to the silver screen. All of them had many scenes that took place in the kitchen. These spaces came complete with pantries and larders, which most kitchens had in days gone by. The pantry would have been used for dry goods as well as silverware and linens, whereas the larder was a cool room in which food was stored. Nowadays, the term "pantry" encompasses both.

Pantries are becoming popular again today and I do not know what I would do without mine. It does away with the need for many extra cabinets in the kitchen and keeps storage out of sight.

Fruit, vegetables and canned preserves are some of the comestibles that are happily ensconced in this precious room, along with extra dishes. Freshly baked pies are allowed to cool on a slate shelf, while potatoes and onions stay fresh in a dark corner.

A pantry does not have to occupy a whole room; take a careful look around near your kitchen and see where you can utilize some space. In my childhood home, my father built a wall of shelves into the nook that led down into the basement. The box-like shelves were just wide enough to hold cans and jars, with curtain wire attached to make sure they did not fall off. Nowadays, 50 years later, the shelves are as useful as ever.

My friends Chris and Kathy, who live in New York, traded their coat cupboard to create a pantry. Their coats now hang from lovely hooks by their front door, which is so much more convenient. Their former coat cupboard is now equipped with deep shelves that meet all their pantry needs.

Pantry style ideas

Nach deutscher Hausfrau'n Sitte

BOXING CLEVER I love using old wooden boxes for storage, especially ones with their original labels intact. They create a neat and ordered space that is a joy to look upon. Mine hold everything from spices to spare jam-jar lids and they are always ready for when I need them.

SHELF IMPROVEMENT In the 19th century, many humble homesteads saved simple scraps of brown paper. These were then cut into various designs to add warmth and character to the edging of shelves. I have edged the shelves in my pantry with vintage homemade fabric edging, which I received as a present – I could not believe how perfectly it fit. Similar trims can be found quite easily at fairs and markets. Long ago, they were often used to decorate kitchens or shelves in cupboards and glass-fronted cabinets. The edging lends an old-fashioned charm to this room.

"A pantry will provide ample storage space and keep your kitchen free from clutter."

UP, UP AND AWAY There is no doubt that there will be a shelf that is far too high to reach without a stool. Make sure this is where you store things that are not needed on a daily basis. I found a wine rack that was the perfect size to store all my wine and cordial bottles.

HANGING BASKET If space allows, try to hang a wire basket where you can store bananas or avocados away from other fruit and vegetables. As long as you keep the space well organized, a pantry will provide you with ample storage space and keep your main kitchen tidy and free from clutter. It complements my unfitted cottage kitchen.

PRIZED DRAWERS I have managed to fit a little set of drawers into my pantry, which is very helpful for storage. If this is not possible, you can always make another curtain to hid bulky items. This is done exactly like the curtain to hide the dishwasher (see page 49).

USEFUL AND BEAUTIFUL I have attached several hooks to the walls of my pantry, where I hang up my cooling trays and anything else that is oddly shaped and difficult to store. The wirework trays were made in the 19th century. Suspending them from hooks ensures their beauty can be enjoyed and that no shelf space is wasted.

Make ideas

Chalkboard

In my pantry, I have painted a simple chalkboard that I attached to the door. Here I quickly scribble items that are required. I use a small enamel bowl on a nearby shelf for my chalk. On grocery shopping days, the list will be compiled from the items on the chalkboard. Either buy a little chalkboard to fit your door or simply paint a rectangular piece of wood with chalkboard paint. Attach it to the door and decorate it in your own style as you see fit. The checked pattern around the border was very simply done using white paint and a piece of sponge.

MATERIALS
sponge • scissors • white paint • chalkboard

1 Cut the sponge into a small square. Dip one side into some white paint and gently dab it around the edge of the chalkboard in a checkerboard design.

2 Continue all the way around until you like your design. Let it dry before hanging the chalkboard in your pantry.

Dish Towel Drawstring Bag

These little bags are invaluable and can be made very quickly. They are useful for storing food that needs to be kept in the dark. I also use mine to hold clean pieces of cloth that I keep on hand to cover food in the fridge.

MATERIALS
tea towel • needle and thread • ribbon or string • safety pin • fabric scissors

1 Fold your dish towel in half with the right side facing inward. Stitch down the side and along the base, leaving an opening at the top.

2 Turn the bag inside out so that the right side is now facing outward.

3 Take the top of the bag and fold it over by 1in/ 2.5cm to create the channel for your string or ribbon. The wrong side of the dish towel will show at the top – for this reason I tend to use gingham towels, which look sweet on both sides. Note that there is an opening where you will be able to thread your ribbon or string.

4 Should you prefer a frill at the top of the bag, simply sew another seam above the first one, leaving enough room to thread your ribbon through. Once, gathered, it will create a lovely ruffle. Pin the fold in place, then stitch around the bag to make your channel.

5 Turn the bag inside out and thread some ribbon or string through the casing. The easiest way to do this is to take a safety pin, attach it to the ribbon and thread it through the channel. When both sides are showing the ribbon, make a knot so that it will not slip back through the casing.

6 If you are making one of these as a present, you could decorate it with some embroidery.

CHAPTER 4

SERVE:
the dining room

In days gone by, a grand dining room might have been used only for special occasions. Today, many houses do not even have such a room, as the kitchen is able to fit a table and chairs. However, our cottage is old enough to have a dining room, and we love to gather round the old Irish pine table. This wonderful piece could tell many stories. A dining room can have plenty of uses, whether it be eating a meal, crafting, doing homework or writing a book.

BELOW *I imagine that this pint-sized chair once belonged to a little girl, who would pull it up to an equally small table for tea parties. I use it for seasonal displays. I made this hand-stitched lavender pillow out of an old quilt as a project for The Cozy Club. Soon, a little pumpkin will take its place.*

RIGHT *I found this old French cupboard at Ardingly Antiques Fair. My heart stood still and I knew at once where it would live in my home. Soon afterward, Caroline Zoob came to do a photo shoot for a book. She asked if she could make little curtains for the cupboard. How could I refuse?*

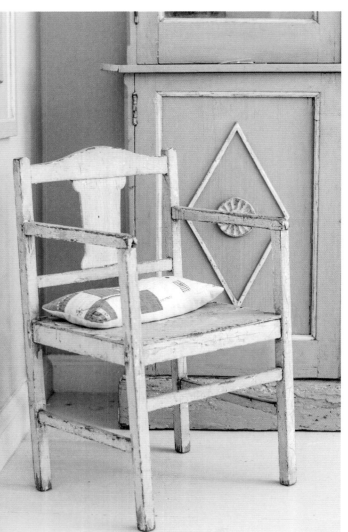

Formal dining-room furniture seems to be slipping into the history books and new, more casual and comfortable furniture is taking its place, promoting a warm and friendly atmosphere. Mismatched chairs, which can be unified by painting them the same color, sit cozily around the table. Pillows are added for comfort to encourage guests to linger for long discussions after the meal is finished.

Rather than using overhead electric lighting, which can be too harsh, think about using lamps and candlelight to establish a soft glow. I so enjoy a chandelier with candles. It looks so beautiful and makes every meal special, as do flickering tealights sprinkled throughout the room. I painted the previously dark floor in our dining room a warm shade of white and slowly a new room emerged, one that is used on a daily basis rather than only once in a while.

The outside world can add so much beauty to this area and bringing in foraged elements is a wonderful way to forge a connection to the changing seasons.

OPPOSITE *The brightly colored flowers on the table draw in all of the hues of the surrounding room, creating a delightful focal point. The tablecloth is actually an old linen sheet, while gingham seat pads on the painted chairs keep the area from becoming too formal.*

"Fill old watering cans and buckets with the bounty that summer brings."

This old galvanized bucket normally lives outside, so it has a charmingly worn and battered appearance. At other times it welcomes visitors into my dining room, where I use it to display a seasonal mix of dainty flowers from my garden.

TOP ROW *Homemade items in every room, such as this stitchery made from an old quilt, announce to all that this is a warm and inviting area. An old sage green painted Canadian lunchbox is in constant use as a vessel to hold cut flowers. The dining room still has its old original windows, so these sweet floral curtains are lined with thick blankets to keep out the chill.*

BOTTOM ROW *My blue-and-white tea set was found at a charity shop a few years ago. The teapot is chipped and the set is not complete, but its patina shows how much it has been loved. This beaded bag was my grandmother's. It would have hung on her wrist while at a dance 100 years ago. Its presence reminds me of her and allows me to pass on her stories.*

Simply adding a ring of ivy upon the chandelier with perhaps a few crimson rosehips tied carefully among the tendrils, will welcome in the winter months. Large pitchers of Queen Anne's lace/cow parsley help usher in spring. Take old, battered watering cans and buckets and fill them with the bounty that summer brings. Equally, the autumn can be celebrated using bowls filled with horse chestnuts and pumpkins.

Use what you have and, with a little imagination, you will be surprised by just how quickly you can change the look of your dining room.

Dining room style ideas

PULL UP A CHAIR Mismatched chairs are just delightful to me. It is a joy to go to a fair or flea market and see a single, beautiful chair just waiting for me. Home it comes to receive a coat or two of paint and then it is welcomed into the chair family. Obviously, comfort is important, so do try out every chair before you buy. And if you are looking for chairs, measure a comfortable height for your table and keep this in mind when hunting for treasures. Often, old chairs and tables will have spent many years in farmhouses, some with dirt floors. Their legs would be cut down as the wood deteriorated, so be mindful of this. This problem is quite easy to fix on a table using blocks, but this will not work for chair legs.

WINDOW DRESSING Do not feel that every window needs the same treatment. My dining room has a small side window and I have just added a sweet frill of gingham to the top of it using curtain wire. It adds charm and a little color while letting in light. In the evenings, a candle glows on the windowsill.

LIFTING THE LID Old trunks and blanket boxes are lovely to look at and can hold off-season decor and scraps of fabric. I have quite a selection of them in my house, including several in the dining room. Placed under tables, they hide electrical sockets really well.

GATHER ROUND There is no need for a large table if you do not have the room. If you are having a big gathering, simply push two smaller tables together and unify them by how you decorate. A tablecloth and a large floral centerpiece, or a row of glass jars holding smaller sprigs down the middle of both tables, will work perfectly to welcome all to the room.

ECLECTIC PERFECTION All of my furniture within this room comes from different time periods and countries: Ireland, Sweden, France and England are all represented. Mixing different styles not only adds interest, it allows you free rein to purchase items that you love. There is no rule that says everything must match. As with the chairs, as long as the colors blend well together, the room will flow. Miraculously, some of the pieces that I have found at fairs were already painted in shades that would suit the room. Whenever this happens, it affirms my claim to myself that this item is destined to come home with me.

STITCHES IN TIME Hang pictures that have a recurring theme. My dining room doubles as my workshop, so I have chosen lovely old samplers to hang about the room. They are a constant source of inspiration to those who are crafting and are also admired during dinner parties as well. My husband made their simple frames using recycled wood, and I have painted them all the same color, which helps keep the room calm and serene.

Make ideas

Picket Fence Pelmet

Years ago I had thick curtains with a frilly pelmet, which looked rather heavy. I asked my husband to make a new pelmet using leftover wood from an old picket fence. It made such a difference to the room. The formal air was instantly diffused by the quirkiness of the pelmet. I painted it to blend into the walls and it works so well.

MATERIALS
wooden batons • saw • picket fence posts • screws • screwdriver • 10 small L brackets • paint • paintbrush

1 Measure the width of the window and add on 2½in/6cm on each side. Cut two wooden batons to that length. Measure the width of a fence post and multiply it by four. Cut four pieces of baton to this length.

2 Cut all the fence posts to the length you desire. Take one and attach it to the two longer batons using two screws, one in each baton. Repeat with the other fence posts along the full length of the batons. You will need eight more fence posts to complete the pelmet.

3 Attach one L bracket to each long baton on either side, four in total.

4 Affix each of the shorter batons to the other side of one of the four L brackets and place four picket pieces on either side, attaching them with screws as before.

5 Attach the pelmet to the wall above the window by using four L brackets, one on each short baton, and place the two remaining L brackets on either side to attach it to the ceiling above.

6 Paint your new pelmet in the color of your choice.

See pages 64–65

Chandelier Decoration

Nothing says celebration more than a room filled with the beauty of flowers. There is no need to rush out to a shop. Just go outside for a walk and look carefully at what nature has to offer. Holly and ivy are ideal in the winter months, but ivy should not be relegated to winter only. It thrives in all seasons and is a great base for any decoration. Add a circlet of ivy to your chandelier and tie on blooms such as hydrangea, lavender and nepeta. Make sure you choose plants that can withstand being out of water for some time. Nigella is perfect and the frothiness of the flowers makes a wonderful summertime statement. Do not be tempted to use plastic flowers!

MATERIALS
ivy • seasonal flower blossoms • floristry wire • flower scissors

1 Gather ivy and your choice of flowers, such as nepeta, dianthus, nigella, clematis, hydrangea and lavender.

2 Add the ivy to your chandelier first, using floristry wire to secure it.

3 Dot the flowers here and there until you are happy with the design. It would be a good idea to let this be your last job before your dinner so that the flowers are at their freshest.

CHAPTER 5

RELAX:
the living room

A living room is what the name implies: a room to live in. I find a room that is used on a regular basis is best decorated in neutral shades with wooden floors and furnished with items that are comfortable and well-loved. Then you can add decorative elements that reflect the seasons. It should not be a pristine space that is hardly used. A living room that is cozy, functional and simple will invite friends and family to sit down and enjoy spending time together.

Only a few main design elements are needed: a comfortable sofa or two, a spot to put down refreshment and proper lighting for reading, with perhaps an armchair to snuggle into. If you're lucky enough to have a fireplace in this room, it is lovely for this to be a focal point.

I do not like to see a television in my living room, although it is the place where we gather to watch movies on stormy nights. As with my dishwasher, I simply made a curtain to hide the screen (see page 49). I admit that there was dissent among the family when I introduced this idea. However, I persevered and now that opening the curtain to watch the television has become a habit, I think they secretly agree with me.

Changing throw pillows or curtains to suit what is happening in nature is a wonderful way to honor the yearly cycle and is a delight to me and my senses. As the weather changes, so do my fabrics. Warm woollens, thick quilts and eiderdowns are aired and made ready for the autumn and winter. During the spring and summer months, the room becomes airy and clean. I love using old linen and worn quilts throughout my home and certainly do not mind if they are mended or threadbare. They tell a delightful story every time I hold them.

ABOVE *I became a grandmother to a little girl named Cecily last year. I could not resist acquiring a pretty rose-colored tea set so that she and I can have many teatimes together. Little hands have played with this set since about 1840.*

OPPOSITE *Having a fireplace is lovely, but when it is not in use during the warmer months of the year, staring into a huge black hole is not ideal. To make it more welcoming, simply add a painted bucket containing a flowering plant. I like to change the plant from time to time.*

In summer, there is very little upkeep and maintenance needed. This is when the outside is welcomed into the living room and the indoors and outdoors almost merge together. I do, however, have a lovely old basket tucked beside my sofa in the warmer months just in case the night air brings a chill and I need to ward off the cold. Candles predominate in all seasons – the warm glow of a small flame, positioned carefully here and there, never fails to bring on a cozy feeling, especially in the evening.

I have a love of old books, particularly old books about Canada, and especially ones that have a dated inscription therein. My mother always told me that books anchor a room – this is particularly important in a living room. Throughout the seasons, I will showcase various titles to complement the time of year. One summer, a few years ago, I had the nicest experience in a second-hand bookstore in a seaside village. Something magical happens when you push open an old pine door and a little jingle announces your presence.

OPPOSITE *Quilts feature in every room of my home. They bring warmth and look lovely displayed here and there. The squares of various fabrics are so delightful and I find that they sit beside other patterns within a room perfectly. Not only pretty, quilts also ward off any chills that the evening may bring.*

RIGHT *Having worked as a librarian for many years, my love of books has never waned. I have enjoyed buying vintage books for as long as I can remember. My favorite collection is by the author LM Montgomery, whose* Anne of Green Gables *stories are a timeless treat.*

"My mother always told me that books anchor a room – this is particularly important in a living room."

OPPOSITE *This lovely house started life as a simple box. As my collection of little mice (not real ones!) began to grow, my husband decided that it was time to find a home for them. He used only reclaimed pieces of wood, many with chipped paintwork, to make the house appear vintage. It gives all who visit no end of pleasure.*

ABOVE LEFT *I have eiderdowns scattered throughout my cottage. These feather-filled covers are a delight to snuggle into on chilly nights, and they are welcoming to see peeking out from a corner of the room.*

ABOVE RIGHT *The covers of my Anne of Green Gables books are worn from use and are a delight to see sprinkled around my room. I love to pick them up on a whim and read a few chapters. Although I know the stories off by heart, just holding the books gives me the most wonderful cozy feeling.*

The strong hot sunshine of the day turned into a world of shadows and dusty corners as I walked into the store. The scent of old paper and the air of forgotten memories stirred my soul and the excitement of what may be found grabbed my imagination. I had entered a world of stories: row upon row of books just waiting to be visited. The shelves were neatly labeled and here and there were small decorative items that, when I asked the owner, proved to be mementos that reminded him of his family and friends.

My first question is always: "Are there any old copies of *Anne of Green Gables* by LM Montgomery?" The gentleman thought for a minute, then hobbled over to the children's section. He looked hard, but then lifted his head saying that he thought he had one but it must have been sold. I told him it is all about the thrill of the hunt. Next time, perhaps. Noting my accent, he asked where I was from. Upon hearing "Canada", his smile broadened, and he reached up and clasped a book.

LEFT *This adorable glass bottle attached to an old painted board with a heart-shaped cutout was a project in my book* Seasonal Scandi Crafts. *Blooms are so important in a cozy cottage and having a little spot upon a wall to display a sprig or two is lovely.*

ABOVE & OPPOSITE *My pigeonhole display houses my collection of small items. This was not painted when I found it but I decided that it needed a lick of paint so that it would be easier to see the objects displayed within. It is a delight to style for the seasons.*

I walked out with a beautiful volume to add to my old Canadian collection. Who would have thought that in a little store like this such treasure could be found? It is these personal experiences that give your home a cozy feeling unique to only you. The passion of collecting and displaying these treasures, from lichen-covered twigs to old books, provides the essence of a natural home. A feeling of simplicity and serenity will permeate every

nook and cranny of your home and provide comfort and interest to all those who visit.

A lovely idea that has been handed down through the generations in our family is to place favorite greetings cards received over the years for various occasions in these old books. They topple out periodically as the books are opened and always bring back a flood of memories.

Living room style ideas

SECOND-HAND STORAGE Most of my furnishings are second-hand or inherited, with a smattering of pieces collected at various brocantes or antique fairs. Before you set out, remember to measure the space that you want to fill and then do not forget to bring along your tape measure.

Storage is a never-ending problem for most people and I am often asked where I put all my cozy collections for each season. I do not have an attic or basement so old trunks, blanket boxes, baskets and worn leather suitcases come into their own for this purpose. Putting away cherished items from season to season allows for a new look and it is exciting to be reunited with treasures that have lain dormant for months, before being unveiled to delight once again. Memories are rekindled as you hold these objects and arranging everything just as you like will make your home look fresh and revived.

All these collections create a space that is personal to you. I have a number of old tin buckets that I use for flowers, pinecones, kindling and such like. They provide a use and are extremely decorative – the more worn the better, in my opinion.

A NATURAL SELECTION

Adding foraged elements into your decorating, such as flowers and greenery, is both economical and friendly to nature. Making your own wreaths and adding branches and stones in a pleasing way is a wonderful pastime. When they are past their prime, you can place them on the compost pile and go out to gather something else.

WHERE THE HEARTH IS A fireplace offers the opportunity to turn a chilly day into a reason to sit and get cozy. If you have one in your home, count your blessings. The mantel can provide a continually changing vista as you add foraged decorations from nature.

If you do not have a fireplace, there are ways to get that same ambience without a real fire. When you are next on a jolly day out, try and find a reclaimed mantel. You can then attach it carefully to the wall. Paint the fixings the same color as your wall so that they disappear from sight, then paint the inside wall black where the grate would have been. Make a simple hearth by laying some bricks against the wall and decorate with logs and baskets of kindling. Create an area in front of the fireplace that is safe to house tealights, or simply drape twinkle lights around to mimic a fire.

A NEW PURPOSE If you are like me, you have tealights tucked away in baskets and beautifully scented candles ready to glow as required. Many candles come in pretty jars and I enjoy reusing them. An easy way to remove the leftover wax is to place the jar in the freezer for an hour or so. Gently tap it and the wax will come away. Use the remnants to make wax melts (see below).

MAKE DO AND MELT Instead of freezing the jars (see above), you can place them in a pan of hot water. Once the wax is liquid, pour it into little French bakery molds or small metal containers. Freeze for about an hour to make wax melts. I have an old copper teapot warmer that belonged to a favorite aunt. I use it both to warm a small teapot and to heat my wax melts. As the wax softens, the delicious fragrance drifts into the air once again.

TREADING THE BOARDS A long time ago, I decided that wall-to-wall carpeting was not for me. As time went by, one room followed another, culminating in the staircase. For the most part, the old pine floorboards were in good condition. If you do the same, you may find some glue left from the carpets and more often than not, the wood is painted with a black or dark brown stain. The rules say that you must sand the boards, then add an undercoat and then paint, but I did not do this.

I tried my best to scrape off the areas that had deposits of old glue. As for the dark paint, I painted over it. Of course, if you want the original flooring left bare, you will have to sand and seal it properly. I envisioned every room and staircase having a warm white painted floor that would be easy to maintain. Take your time on this job – I painted each plank twice, leaving the first coat to dry for at least a few days before adding the next layer. From time to time, I may repaint an area that receives a lot of wear and tear, but the odd mark here and there does not bother me at all. Any good-quality floor paint will do the job nicely.

Make ideas

Weathered Seaglass Wreath

My mother has collected seaglass for as long as I can remember. On the shores of Lake Huron in Canada, it always felt like finding treasure whenever a sliver of worn glass appeared in the sand. Her friend made her a sweet, simple wreath from found glass a few years ago. It serves as a lovely reminder of past summers.

MATERIALS
seaglass, softly worn with no sharp edges (or use pretty pebbles, small pinecones or dried flowers) · small grapevine wreath or thick wire circle · ribbon or string · hot glue gun

1 Gather together all the seaglass.

2 Take your wreath base and tie on a piece of ribbon or string for the hanger.

3 Using a hot glue gun, simply adhere the pieces of glass in a pleasing shape around the wreath. Stop from time to time to consider your next placement.

4 Let the glue dry, then hang up your wreath to remind you of a sunny summer's day.

Spindle Candleholders

Walking through a lovely antique store, filled with items that have their own history and secret story to tell, is something that is very special to me. Imagining all of these pieces being useful so many years ago yet still remaining intact today is quite wonderful.

While antiquing one day, we happened upon an architectural salvage yard, where we found an assortment of staircase pieces just waiting patiently to be used once again. We took home a spindle with absolutely no idea what we would do with it, but an idea soon presented itself. In no time, the spindle was transformed into a pair of striking candleholders. They now stand regally on my mantel and lend themselves to being decorated for all the seasons.

MATERIALS
old staircase spindle · saw · sandpaper · drill (optional) · aluminum foil · two tapered candles or tealights · PVA glue · two pieces of thin wood, both 5in/12.5cm square

1 Cut the spindle precisely in half at 90 degrees so that the two pieces are symmetrical. Sand down all the cut edges.

2 Take one spindle piece and drill a hole, a little wider than one of the tapered candles, approximately ½in/1cm deep into the top where you want the candle to rest. Line the hole with foil so that the candle does not scorch the wood when it burns down.

3 Repeat with the other piece. Should you not wish to drill, you can simply rest a tealight on top of the spindle.

4 Glue the cut edge of each spindle piece on your base and make sure there is good adhesion. Leave to dry before adding candles or tealights.

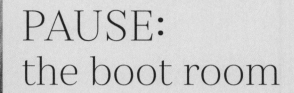

CHAPTER 6

PAUSE: the boot room

A boot room is most definitely a bonus if you have the space. It is a place to hide your muddy boots, washing machine, tool kit and recycling area with plenty of mismatched hooks to hang coats and cleaning tools. I waited for quite a few years before I managed to find a designated area and it is simply wonderful. However, there are ways that you can make a boot room by carving out a hidden spot in your home.

I can almost guarantee that you have a place that is hardly ever used where you could design a space. It might be the space under the stairs, a cupboard or simply a nook. All you really need to do is add a few shelves, some wicker baskets to hold all of your recycling and some lovely worn apple crates for shoes and your boot room will be ready to go.

I love the look of cleaning brushes hanging from old hooks. I also have a vintage basket where I stash my jars of homemade cleaning mixtures. It is amazing what you do not need in your cleaning cupboard. I have long been an advocate of natural cleaning products after spending time reading what the plastic spray bottles contain. I researched for quite some time and read copious books on the subject. What these authors and I have in common is that we do not wish to use anything that is harmful to us, our families or the environment. You only need a few basic ingredients in order to make cleaning easy and non-toxic. Once you start on this path, you will wonder why it took you so long.

ABOVE *Corner shelves and vintage drawers are ideal in a small space. Add a set of little drawers to add a warm vintage feel to the room. Mason jars and amber-colored glass bottles make great containers for homemade cleaning products (see page 94) and dried rose petals (see page 171).*

FAR LEFT AND LEFT *Wire baskets are easy to attach to a wall, freeing up space on the worktop. I like having my cleaning utensils and scissors close to hand; also, brushes kept in the open will dry rapidly, prolonging their lifespan.*

This sink with its wall-mounted faucets/taps is minute in size, but it does all that it needs to do. Muddy boots are quickly cleaned, and laundry can be soaked with ease. Storage is concealed simply by attaching a small gathered curtain below the sink (see page 49).

> "Plastic bags are a thing of the past – I have a stash of fabric bags hanging by the door."

Boot room style ideas

PROTECTING THE PLANET Even as a little girl, I always preferred things made from natural materials or found in the great outdoors. We all now know that plastic is detrimental to the environment and, thanks to Sir David Attenborough and others, it is so wonderful to see that the world is waking up to this crisis. To keep your home as plastic free as possible, I think you have to look back to see how things were done many years ago. Plastic wrap/clingfilm may make storing food quick and easy, but you do not need it in your home at all. Thankfully, there are now items on the market such as beeswax-coated fabric wraps and elasticated fabric covers that do the same job. I also recommend investing in pots and pans with lids. If you need a lid and don't have one to hand, simply lay a clean cloth over a dish and lay a plate on top to cover the contents.

BEYOND PLASTIC Plastic bags are becoming a thing of the past. Growing up, I witnessed my mother heading out to the shops with a fabric bag or two tucked into her purse. When she arrived home, these bags were emptied and folded away to be used another day. She did this without thinking as her mother had taught her. How did we lose this simple idea over the years? Luckily we are all back on board and all you need to do is remember to bring your bags with you. I always have a stash of fabric bags hanging by the door. I keep small paper bags handy to take along as well to house the loose vegetables I buy. Above all, I really hate waste of any kind. Be careful when going grocery shopping. Special offers such as two-for-one deals are not so special if you buy more than you need only to throw it out. Think carefully before you go shopping, make a list and stick to it as much as possible.

BRICK BY BRICK The floor of my boot room is made of simple bricks. Over the years, they had become stained and no amount of scrubbing made them look clean. Finally, I grabbed some leftover paint and slapped it over the bricks. It took about 15 minutes, but what a transformation. I wondered how long this would last and if the painted bricks would be easier to clean. I am happy to report that not only are they clean but the room itself looks brighter. Sometimes there is no need to overthink a problem and my advice to you is to take the bull by the horns and move forward.

THE SCENT OF CINNAMON Many wonderful ideas are serendipitous. Once, I reached for my large tin of cinnamon and then all of a sudden I somehow slipped and about two tablespoons spilled on the floor. As cinnamon is so fine, I thought it best to get out the vacuum cleaner to tidy it up. The following day, I used the vacuum again and the delightful scent of cinnamon drifted through the air once again. Each time I used it the same thing happened, the gorgeous fragrance of cinnamon dissipated into the air. Now, whenever I change my vacuum cleaner bags, I add a large dash of cinnamon into the fresh bag. It certainly makes vacuum cleaning so much nicer and the lingering scent of cinnamon is such a treat.

NEAT AND TIDY In my boot room I store my recycling baskets, my kitchen linen and my laundry machines. As with the rest of my house, I do not like to see the appliances. I have made a curtain for them the same way I did for the dishwasher in my kitchen (see page 49). I have a little butler's sink and an old cupboard that holds all my bulk cleaning items as well as my ever-growing collection of dish towels. There is something very satisfying about opening a cupboard and seeing a neat stack of towels looking back at you. Add to that my natural cleaning products and a few pitchers for flowers and I feel quite content. I have an air dryer on hand, as I prefer to dry my clothes outside if possible. If the weather does not permit, I leave them in the warm kitchen overnight instead.

Make ideas

Baking Soda

I always keep a jar of baking soda handy next to the sink. A teaspoon or two sprinkled onto very dirty dishes does wonders, and a paste of baking soda and water is a fantastic cleaning agent for your oven and stovetop. To keep drains clean, combine half a cup of baking soda, half a cup of vinegar and a dash of salt. Pour this down the drain, followed by some boiling water.

Old china and glass sometimes become yellowed or clouded with age. Simply rub the china with the baking soda paste and the yellow sheen disappears. As for the cloudy glass, cut up a raw potato and rub it on the surface, then rinse. Your glass will shine once

Vinegar

Vinegar is really the ultimate natural cleaning solution to have in your cupboard. If you like to rinse your dishes to make them spotless and sparkling, add a dash of vinegar to the water. To make a general surface cleaner, add a cup of vinegar into a bucket of warm water or use one part vinegar to four parts water in a spray bottle. To add luster to your windows, spray this mixture onto the glass and wipe dry with newspaper.

Wood Burner

Often the glass in a wood-burning stove blackens with soot. The easiest way to clean this is with wet newspaper and cold ashes from the fire. The ash acts as a scrub and cleans the glass as if by magic. The idea was given to me by a delightful older gentleman from whom we purchased a wood burner for our cottage in Canada. It is the best example of recycling I have ever seen.

Natural Dish Soap

After trying many recipes and adding my own ideas, I have created what I think is an effective and safe mixture. The recipes that I tried out did not get the results that I wanted. I have created my own version to get the most cinnamon fragrance when washing dishes and also getting suds to form. It feels lovely stirring the few ingredients together knowing that it is all natural and safe to use. You can purchase all the ingredients online or at a health food store.

MATERIALS
½ cup warm water • 2 teaspoons salt • ½ cup Dr Bronner's Sal Suds biodegradable cleaner • pump bottle • cinnamon essential oil

1 Mix the salt in the water until dissolved (the salt will make the mixture thicker). Add the Sal Suds and stir. The mixture will go cloudy and thicken slightly.

2 Pour the dish soap into your bottle ready to be used. You only need a pump or two for a sink full of water. It does not make as many suds as your everyday dish soap, but it is not the suds that make things clean.

3 Other recipes say to add the essential oil to the mixture. However, I have found that the scent is better, and the bottle of essential oil lasts longer, if you just put a few drops into your sink as you are filling it. The warmth of the water will release the scent of cinnamon.

CHAPTER 7

DREAM: the bedroom

For most people, the bedroom is a private space made to enjoy with those closest to you. It is so important to create an environment that is both serene and relaxing. Your bed must be chosen with care, and the linens with which you surround yourself will feel most wonderful when made from natural materials such as cotton, linen and wool. All three get better with age and, if cared for properly, last for a long time. They are also soft against the skin.

RIGHT *Making sure that all the windows of your home have the appropriate curtains can be daunting. Remember, all windows do not need heavy coverings. I love the view from my attic window and do not want to obscure the outlook. I decided to add just a little frill of fabric to add a touch of warmth to the window.*

FAR RIGHT *A pretty eiderdown looks sweet adorning a linen cover on a bed. These humble coverings filled with natural down create a certain ambiance within the bedroom. The layering of the two covers provides warmth when in use and the enchanting fabric of the eiderdown brings subtle color to the bedding.*

I do not feel the need to iron my bed linen. A few wrinkles only enhance the coziness of the bed and make it more inviting. I enjoy a thick feather duvet in the autumn and winter and during the warmer months I layer old quilts and blankets over my sheets should the evening turn cool.

It is said that reading before lights out sends you to sleep naturally. A bedside table, if you have the space, is an ideal place to store your books and perhaps a posy of flowers to lightly scent the night air. Should space be tight, a little fabric bag held in place tucked under the mattress can act as a catch-all for glasses and books (see page 112). It is simple to make and great if you have limited space by your bedside.

A good night's sleep is achieved by having a fresh breeze to cool and calm and then being woken naturally by the sun. Hot summers may entice you to turn on the air conditioning, but try a fan instead. The soft whirring sound is much nicer than the hum of artificial cold blasts. If it is really hot, take a cool shower before bed.

LEFT *I love all quilts. Being Canadian, I find red and white ones most appealing. Draping quilts over beds and sofas adds instant warmth and brings the past to life. When I look at the stitching, it is hard to fathom the work and time involved in creating such a masterpiece by hand.*

LEFT My friend Lynne called me not too long ago with the news that she had found an old pine door in a skip that might be of interest to me. She knew that we had wanted to exchange our modern doors for ones more in keeping with the house. My husband made the switch. There is no need for me to tell you how happy I am with the result!

BELOW LEFT Look out at fairs for treasures that others may overlook. Worn-out quilts often have areas that can be salvaged and used to make pillow covers and other homewares.

BELOW Finding an old trunk in a little antique store is always exciting. Imagine my excitement when I opened this one and found that the interior had been covered in an exquisite rose wallpaper. This had begun to peel, revealing a pattern of little stars on the paper beneath. There was no question that it was coming home with me.

"Old toys are not just for show but are to be loved by future generations."

THIS PAGE & OPPOSITE TOP *This little room holds a collection of cherished items perfect for make-believe. The dollhouse is home to a family of mice. Rabbits and dolls sit ready to be played with, while a trio of tins holds small toys and games. The antique sleigh bed is topped with a heap of eiderdowns and a jumble of throw pillows. Old boxes slip easily under the bed for handy storage.*

Simple window coverings add to the feeling of calm in the bedroom. I have a small dormer window, for which I made a roll-up shade/blind that I can hang at different levels to let in as much or as little light as I wish (see page 112).

Guest bedrooms have the same requirements, but added touches are always appreciated. Extra pillows and blankets, fresh flowers and plenty of reading material are essential. Add a pitcher of water and a bundle of towels, and your guests may never want to leave.

BELOW LEFT & RIGHT *Memories are so important in a home. This framed stitchery was made by my dear friend Jo. The frame was created by my husband and the chipped paintwork on the reclaimed wood picks up the colors of*

the threads beautifully. Both the work and its frame are reminders of very special people and add personality to my home. Meanwhile, the little fellows sitting on a shelf simply make me smile – this is exactly what a cozy cottage should do.

LEFT *The green color of the walls in the nursery enhances the soft shade of red in the soft furnishings. The little rabbits wait patiently for a playmate. Although our spare bedrooms do not see everyday use, there is much joy in filling them with fresh flowers from time to time.*

OPPOSITE *The sweet stitched pictures just seen beside the window are two sections of an old baby blanket that once belonged to the dearest of men, Tom Lawrence. Decorating a home should come from the heart. Each item should have meaning and a memory. By curating your interiors with this ethos in mind, you will naturally create a cozy home that is filled with warmth, love and contentment.*

RIGHT *These gorgeous Norwegian sweaters were made for children who are now grown with children of their own. Their mother gave them to me when my boys were little. They remind me of this dear family and the many memories that we have together. I look forward to passing them onto my grandchildren.*

FAR RIGHT *Look around your home for extra storage space. I have many baskets of varying sizes because they have so many uses. Large ones often find a home under beds.*

Bedroom style ideas

HAVE A SEAT Your bedroom should be treated as an oasis, where you can leave the world behind for a spell. Set aside a corner of your room where you can take some time to completely relax until you are ready to greet the day. Add a comfortable chair or sofa and have a small table nearby where you can display a selection of books and magazines along with a little jar of flowers that are in season. Just arranging this space will make you feel incredibly lighthearted.

"Set aside a corner where you can take some time to relax until you are ready to greet the day."

A NEW LEASE OF LIFE Bedrooms, like the rest of a home, go through many changes over the years. Two of the bedrooms in my house once belonged to my boys. The day that each moved out was, of course, hard on my heart. The way I dealt with it was to clean their rooms from top to bottom. Once they looked as they should, I closed the door. As time went by, I would peek into these rooms and reminisce.

One day I decided enough was enough and started to redecorate. The boys did not mind in the least and it was great fun. One room has become an extra guest room, while the other has been turned into a nursery for my grandchildren to use when they come to stay.

As luck would have it, I was given two World War One military beds by my friend Denise. Although the nursery was small, I felt that the beds had to stay together, having been a pair for over 100 years. A lot of moving about ensued. What I would suggest when trying to rearrange a room is to take out as much of the furniture as you can and start afresh. It is much easier than moving things around each other. Once the beds found their place, everything else slotted in perfectly.

SOFT FOCUS Every bedroom always needs extra pillows. Add them as you see fit and have fun with the fabrics. A collection of pillows of varying sizes encourages the urge to snuggle in. I suggest you fill these with natural inserts made with either feathers or kapok, a plant-based alternative. Both will keep the pillow fresh and are easily washed. I always cover pillows with two pillowcases, both made of cotton or linen. This protects the pillow more effectively and the two cases can be easily taken off and washed.

A WARM WELCOME A heap of old quilts and blankets to be gathered when needed is not only beautiful to look at, but also useful. Leaving them scattered about in baskets and blanket boxes throughout your home will encourage everyone to cozy up. This holds true when readying a guest room. Leaving a bundle of fresh towels rolled up in a basket near the door is very welcoming. Add to this a jar of homemade bath salts and a fresh cake of soap wrapped in brown parchment paper and string and your guests will know that they have entered into the warm hug of your home.

CHILDHOOD MEMORIES Open shelves to showcase old toys and books are lovely in a bedroom, as is a row of mismatched hooks (see page 112). I have an old French kitchen shelf in the nursery, which spans almost the whole wall. Books, stuffed animals and wooden playthings are constantly being rearranged. The toys, some of which belonged to my parents and grandparents, are not just for show but are to be loved by future generations. They all tell a story and add so much warmth to our home.

SAFELY STOWED Having a built-in linen closet is not always possible, so you must think of other ways to store your extra bedding. First, edit what you already own. I can almost guarantee that you have some items that you never use but cannot throw away. Look at each item carefully. When you have decided which ones should be taken away, check whether they are made from natural fibres. If so, you can cut them up to be placed in your rag bag.

I have a lovely old pine cupboard that holds all my bed linen. I painted the exterior and added some leftover wallpaper on the inside of the cupboard doors, which makes me smile each time I open the doors. I fold everything neatly inside and tuck in some clove-filled fabric bags to deter moths.

FEATHER BEDDING Having an eiderdown at the bottom of the bed may seem a very old-fashioned idea. How they must have kept toes warm in days gone by. Today they hark back to another era, one that seems to have been less frenzied. I think this is why I love them so much. These humble coverings, filled with natural down, create a certain ambience in the bedroom. I always keep a look out for them at fairs and flea markets. They are easy to wash in a machine on a delicate cycle and then you can simply hang them out to dry in the sunshine. To fluff them up once again, simply shake them about to loosen the feathers. Fold them three times lengthways and they look delightful and inviting upon the bed.

FINDING A FIREPLACE If you live in an old house, look carefully at the floors of the bedrooms and see if you can find a hearth. If you see one, then once upon a time there was a fireplace. If you are like me, then you need to investigate and this is where it gets exciting.

When I found an old hearth in my bedroom, I took a sledgehammer and broke away the plaster. A friend of mine came to help, showing me the correct way to do it. First, you must take off the baseboard/skirting board. Gently hit the wall enough to make it break away, then chisel away at it carefully until you have a big enough space to put your hand in under the wall. In my case I let out a yell as I felt an old grate. This was so thrilling.

Once the whole fireplace was uncovered and I had cleaned up the mess (there was a lot of dust, so cover up as much as you can beforehand), my husband made a sweet little surround out of old pine. If your home is new and you want to add the idea of a fireplace in the bedroom, a little mantel found at a fair can look so adorable. Where the grate would be, paint the area black. In front of the pretend fireplace you can add some candles, a little basket of pinecones or a bucket of fresh flowers. Either way, you will have made a cozy addition to the bedroom to encourage sweet dreams.

MAKING THE BED There is no art in making a bed. If you purchase good-quality linens, your bed will look and feel fabulous. I am partial to the odd frill here and there too. I like to have a bed skirt/valance to cover up the base of the bed – it looks so much cozier. Add an old quilt or two, along with an eiderdown, and you could not find a more pleasing spot to lay your head.

"There is no more welcoming a sight than walking into a bedroom made ready for you and bursting with flowers."

FRILL SEEKER When in doubt, add ruffles! I find that adding a simple gathering of fabric adds so much charm to a room. The trick is not to overdo it. A soft frill of fabric falling softly among some pillows is all that is needed to turn an ordinary bed into something extraordinary.

THE PERFECT POSY Flowers always make me happy, so there is no doubt that whenever I get a room ready for my friends, a fresh posy plays an important role. However, many people do have allergies so it is best to ask first if you are not sure. I love to place a jar next to the bed, on the windowsill and anywhere else I feel is necessary. Herbs are also lovely to use – they also last much longer and their scent is delicious. As a guest, there is no more welcoming a sight than walking into a bedroom made ready for you and bursting with flowers.

MIX AND MATCH If hanging space is at a premium, attaching mismatched hooks to bedroom walls and doors will create extra space for guests to hang their clothes. Make sure you add some old wooden hangers as well – there are some lovely examples to be found. Affixing odd hooks to a worn plank of wood looks wonderful, especially if you paint all the hooks the same color (see page 112). I love to hang old blankets and quilts from these hooks when they are not needed for clothes. This simple cottage feature adds real charm to the room.

TIME FOR TEA When you are staying in someone's home, it is nice to feel spoiled. I love bringing guests an early morning cup of tea. If you have guests who prefer to make their own, place a tray set with a little electric kettle, a selection of teas and instant coffee and some homemade biscuits. Should they need milk, I make sure that they take some up in a Thermos the night before. There is nothing quite like tea in bed first thing in the morning, especially when you are away from home. No doubt plans for the day are hatched while enjoying the beverage.

REFLECTIVE CALM A mirror is an essential item to have within any bedroom, and a well-placed one will make the room appear larger. It is helpful, if possible, to place the mirror near a socket in case a hairdryer is required. Place a basket near the mirror with the hairdryer ready to be used and your guests will appreciate your thoughtfulness. There are lovely big old mirrors to be found. Some are very large, but do not dismiss them – they make great statement pieces and look wonderful simply leaned against a wall (secure with a bracket if needed). Also important to realize is that, just because an old mirror may have some de-silvering, this does not mean that it is not usable. I think it is actually more appealing and shows the age of the mirror. Reusing old items is integral to creating a natural cozy home.

Make ideas

Simple Window Shade

Small dormer windows do not allow a lot of light in, so you have to think creatively. I recommend sewing a simple shade/blind that can be rolled up to the top.

MATERIALS
fabric • fabric scissors • needle and thread • curtain wire • wooden dowel • 2 pairs of hooks and eyes • ribbon or fabric to tie up the shade

1 Measure the exact size of the window you want to cover and cut the fabric to the right size, leaving a seam allowance of ½in/1.5cm. Hem all four sides.

2 Make a pocket at the top for the curtain wire and another at the bottom for the dowel will go through. The dowel makes it easier to roll up the shade.

3 Cut the wire and dowel to the right length. Attach the hooks to the window frame and the eyes to the wire.

4 Thread the wire through the upper channel, hang the shade, then thread the dowel through the lower channel.

5 Drape a piece of ribbon evenly over the shade, ready to secure it when rolled up.

See page 110

Bedside Fabric Bag

My grandmother used to put items in need of mending in a fabric bag in her living room. I've made a similar bag in which I can drop my book and glasses by my bed.

MATERIALS
2 pieces of fabric, one measuring 12½ x 8½in/ 32 x 22cm and the other 12½ x 24½in/ 32 x 62cm • needle and thread • sewing machine (optional) • fabric scissors

1 Take the longer piece of fabric and fold over the edges to make a small hem all the way around.

2 Taking the other piece of fabric, hem one of the longer sides, which will form part of the opening of the bag.

3 With right sides facing inward, sew the two pieces together, then turn the bag inside out.

4 Tuck the long flap of fabric under your mattress, so that the bag is hanging securely next to the bed with the opening facing upward. You are now ready to place your items in your bag to keep them safe while you sleep.

Hooks On Old Board

Hooks are very useful and look especially charming when fastened to an old piece of wood. An uneven number of hooks is most pleasing on the eye.

MATERIALS
an uneven number of hooks – I like them to be mismatched • a weathered piece of wood • screwdriver and screws • paint and paintbrush (optional) • measuring tape • anchors/rawlplugs (for a concrete or brick wall) or more screws (for a wooden wall or door)

1 Attach each hook to the piece of wood, starting with one in the middle. They should be equally spaced along the length of the wood.

2 Paint the hooks if you wish.

3 Attach the plank of wood to the inside of any door or a suitable wall.

See page 111

CHAPTER 8

UNWIND: the bathroom

Historically, the bathroom has come a long way. After all, making a privy a cozy place to be was never a priority – rather this room was merely a necessity, relegated to the back of the house. Now, the bathroom is seen as an oasis, an area for relaxation. A brimming tub or a waterfall shower are among life's pleasures. No matter how big or small your bathroom may be, you can create a sanctuary to soothe your soul. I love to place little jars of rosemary and thyme in my bathing area. The warmth in the room releases the scent and the worries of the day instantly melt away.

I find that a pedestal sink is a neat and simple choice in a bathroom. I keep the surrounding area clear and use baskets for storage. I found this old mirror at a brocante. It is worn and the glass is slightly silvered, but I think that just adds to the romance of the room.

ABOVE LEFT *Fresh flowers and a piece of lace, placed on an old French bistro chair beside the tub, bring charm to this room. Add bottles filled with deliciously scented soap and your bathing experience will be magical.*

ABOVE CENTER *This gorgeous rusty chandelier was given to me by my fabulous Aunt Evon. She had it in her garden and noticed how I loved it. It now hangs happily over my tub and each day I smile and think of her as I glance upon this delightful present. It is utterly magical when furnished with tealights.*

ABOVE RIGHT *Pretty baskets come in all shapes and sizes, but I particularly love ones that have had a previous life and display a little wear and tear.*

Try to keep this room as clutter free as possible. Create a calming atmosphere by placing essential items, such as toilet paper and toothpaste, in wicker baskets or wire containers. Amber-colored apothecary jars containing hand soap and shampoo are gorgeous to look at and easy to refill. If you do not have space for baskets, try making fabric storage pockets (see page 123).

There are many lovely soap makers out there who have researched how to create soap that is beautiful to use as well as harmless to nature. Placing these homespun items on a piece of found wood, a flat stone or a vintage soap dish is perfect. I have collected little ceramic cheese strainers to hold my soaps. Some are even in the shape of a heart. The little holes let the water drain away.

As an extra treat, I like to sprinkle dried rose petals (see page 171) in the bathtub along with a few drops of lavender essential oil. This combination makes you feel like you are sinking into tub full of flowers. Lavender is believed to induce a restful sleep as well. During the colder months, I add cinnamon and clove oil to the bath water instead.

Making your own bath salts (see page 123) is a very quick and easy thing to do. They make a wonderful gift when presented in a mason jar and look so pretty sitting on a bathtub tray – a lovely indulgence that is also very good for you. After a bath, wrapping yourself in a thick towel gives you a wonderful feeling of being cocooned. I like to dry my towels outside – the outdoor scent is delicious, and it lingers in the room.

If you are planning to remodel your bathroom, look out for vintage sinks and tubs. Often these old, interesting pieces are much cheaper than buying new and can be restored to create a beautiful focal point for the room.

OPPOSITE *This charming bathroom is tucked up in my attic. The little cast-iron tub fits into the corner and everything needed for a delightful soak is close at hand. Small framed pictures and little tealights placed here and there add to the intimate atmosphere.*

RIGHT *A little wooden shelf under a mirror is very practical. These are quite easy to find at fairs and second-hand stores. Spruce it up with some paint*

and it will be ready to hold a spray of blooms in a sweet little vase and a fresh bar of soap to welcome guests.

BELOW RIGHT *This sweet little picture hangs in my small downstairs bathroom. I found it exactly as you see it more than 30 years ago. It is a delightful stitchery and it just says "home" and "cozy" to me. Even the simplest room in my house is decorated with a small cup of fresh flowers.*

Turning your bathroom into a special area is not hard to do. The adage "less is more" is particularly apt in the smallest room of the house. Candles can add immensely to the atmosphere. Dot tealights along a windowsill or next to the bathtub. Just make sure they are placed in a safe spot and do not forget to blow them out before you leave the room.

In a small room, wallpaper with a large print is quite striking; it envelops you without feeling overwhelming. I have a blousy rose wallpaper in my bathroom and it never fails to make me smile. I papered all the walls, including the ceiling, but the white tiles around the bath and the sink keep the area from becoming too busy. When I noticed water marks on the wallpaper, I mixed some white emulsion with water and carefully painted the area that was stained. It was magic. The stained marks disappeared and now the wallpaper just looks beautifully faded. It was a quick and easy fix and still looks great years later.

Cleaning a bathroom is less of a chore if you have a basket located out of sight filled with homemade cleansers. A mixture of vinegar and water in a glass spray bottle will make mirrors sparkle. To disinfect the area, mix half a cup of baking soda into a bucket of hot water, then use a rag to wipe all the surfaces. I find that if you clean the bathroom often, it is not an unpleasant task at all, especially if you shake a few drops of an essential oil into your cleaning buckets, and it makes the space such a joy to use.

KEEPING IT NEAT
Use wicker and wire
baskets to keep the
room from becoming
too cluttered. Keep
cleansers and rags on
hand for quick and
frequent cleaning.

Bathroom style ideas

A DISH WITH A DIFFERENCE Use old trinket dishes or cheese strainers to house your bars of soap. You can also find vintage enamel soap dishes at fairs and flea markets, which are just wonderful.

CLEAR WINNERS Mason jars are ideal vessels in which to store cotton balls. They look pretty and keep their contents clean and dry. These are easy to find when hunting for treasure at flea markets.

FRESH INSPIRATION Place little jars of herbs and flowers on the sink and bathtub. Not only does this look sweet, it also adds a wonderful scent to the room. Herbs are particularly good, as they last a long time in a vase. I love to use rosemary and thyme.

ON THE TABLE If your bathroom has enough space, place a little table or chair beside the tub as a spot for guests to place their belongings. A small posy of flowers there will be welcome, too.

WITHIN EASY REACH I recommend placing a fabric bag filled with spare rolls of toilet paper on the door handle in the inside of the bathroom. This ensures that no one will be left hunting when the need arises.

HEAVENLY SCENTS Essential oils add instant luxury thanks to their intense fragrance. A few drops are sufficient to scent the whole room. Use different types depending on the season: lavender for summer and cinnamon and clove for the colder months.

WASTE NO WATER Leave an enamel cup near the sink for people to fill up when brushing their teeth rather than leaving the water rushing from the faucet/tap. Water is a precious commodity; it is a shame to waste it.

GET THE GLOW Tealights placed around the bathtub add that feeling of indulgence and encourage relaxation. Lighting them as the tub fills makes you slow down and savor the moment.

Make ideas

Homemade Bath Salts

Delectable bath salts can be quite expensive to buy, but you can make your own with three simple ingredients. They make a delightful present. I like to add a few extra drops of essential oil when I run the bath to fill the room up with the delicious fragrance.

MATERIALS
¼ cup sweet almond oil · 1 cup coarse sea salt · essential oil of your choice · glass jar with lid

1 Mix the almond oil and sea salt together in a bowl.

2 Add a few drops of the essential oil at a time until you have achieved your desired scent.

3 Tip the bath salts into the jar, close the lid and place near the tub. Simply open the jar and scoop out a little with your fingers each time you would like to add some to your bath water.

Homemade Moisturizer

Creating your own body moisturizer and placing it into a lovely old-fashioned jar is extremely satisfying. I often make it with cinnamon essential oil, but lavender or rose oil would be lovely in the summertime.

MATERIALS
1 cup sweet almond oil · essential oil of your choice · amber-colored glass jar with pump attachment

1 Place the sweet almond oil into the jar.

2 Add approximately 12 drops of the essential oil (more if you want a stronger fragrance).

3 Shake the bottle and you are done – I told you it was easy!

Bathroom Storage Pockets

Years ago, it was the norm to have shoe holder pockets in wardrobes and closets. This is a similar idea, but made to hang on the back of a door. The pockets add to the decor of a room and can hold anything from children's treasures to face cloths and hairbrushes.

MATERIALS
20 x 24in/50 x 60cm piece of fabric · 2 strips of fabric to make pockets, each 20 x 8in/50 x 20cm · needle and thread · fabric scissors · ribbon · pins · nails

1 Iron a ½in/1½cm seam allowance around all four sides of the three pieces of fabric. Hem each one, neatly folding the cut edge underneath.

2 Cut three pieces of ribbon the same length to make hanging loops. Sew these to the short edge of the large piece of fabric, two at the ends and one in the middle.

3 Lay the fabric flat on the table and pin on the strips of fabric so that they run parallel to the short edge.

4 Sew the sides and bottom of the strips onto the large piece of fabric to make two pockets.

5 Divide up the pockets by stitching vertically from the top to the bottom of the strips. Make as many of these smaller pockets as you think you will need – think about what you want to store in here and then make the pockets the appropriate size.

CHAPTER 9

INSPIRE: the reading room

One can never have too many books or magazines – the only problem is where to accommodate them. It is a joy to have bookshelves placed throughout your home and filled with a pleasing variety of books. A snug armchair or plump floor pillow is all that is needed to encourage a few minutes of relaxation as you turn the pages of a favorite novel or magazine. The power of the written word to whisk you away into another world can never be overestimated.

The slanting walls of this attic room seem to envelop me when I come here to read or write. The dormer window allows air and light to filter in gently. The walls and ceiling are covered in a sweet floral wallpaper, which has plenty of cottage charm without being overwhelming. The vintage typewriter is used on a regular basis.

RIGHT *A cozy chair with a linen cover is a perfect place to curl up with a book. I chose a simple red gingham fabric for the pillows. The chest of drawers was a second-hand find. Its scalloped base caught my eye. The handles were missing, but it did not take long to get it looking just right. It holds all my wrapping paper – I have spent many joyful hours packaging up presents in this room.*

The attic of a house is normally an ideal area for storage. Some may say that a small space with slanted ceilings is awkward and inconvenient, but I would say that it conjures up images of writers in days gone by, penning their classics by candlelight in little garrets. In my attic, I have created a small, charming and practical room that fills my heart with joy.

This room has served many purposes over the years, having been used as a spare bedroom for little guests and as a sewing area when my boys were young. Now it houses my rather vast collection of magazines and books in the space under the low sloping ceiling, on shelves made from old apple crates and scaffolding boards. Magazines are grouped by genre, with the spines facing outward. From time to time, I spend a few delicious hours sorting through them. Any that I no longer need are shared with others.

As the room is quite small, the wallpaper continues onto the ceiling. It is a flower-filled design that provides a feeling of walking into a secret garden. Although there

is plenty of light thanks to a small window and some spotlights, I prefer using candles here. They create a wonderfully old-fashioned atmosphere that pervades this little room and encourages daydreaming. A small desk provides the perfect spot to pen letters, while a soft chair in the corner invites you to curl up and read. This can make it rather difficult to leave.

Having little souvenirs of the past scattered about in your home will add character. In this room, I have two pairs of woollen slippers that my boys used to wear, which conjure up memories of them as children.

Although you may not be able to devote a specific room in your house to reading and writing, it may be possible to carve out a space in a room already designed for another purpose. The key is to look at your surroundings with fresh eyes. Place a bookshelf in a corner, add a lamp and a comfortable chair or pillow and your reading nook will soon become a reality. One day a room may become available, but do not let it stop you from creating your own secret spot right now.

Reading room style ideas

SIMPLE AND STURDY Slanted ceilings can make furniture arranging difficult, as the ergonomics are somewhat impractical. Practical pieces that can be easily moved and reconfigured will solve many problems and allow you to make the most of the available space. My bookshelves are made from old apple crates and sturdy wooden boards, which are brilliant. They can be put together in combinations of any shape or size, and they are quick to set up and take down. Both the crates and the boards are strong and durable, making them ideal for supporting stacks of heavy books and periodicals.

AN INSPIRING INFUSION It is very important to have refreshments close to hand while reading, writing or daydreaming. I have a tray in my attic that holds everything I need for tea time. My grandfather was in the tea import trade many years ago and he taught my father the joy of freshly brewed loose tea leaves, which my father in turn passed on to me. My preferred blend, a fragrant mixture of Earl Grey, Assam and Darjeeling, is kept in an old tin with a lid. Knowing that I will be spending some time in this room, I take along a pitcher of fresh cold milk and a bottle of water. Nothing is nicer than sitting and reading in the corner of this little room while enjoying a cup of freshly brewed tea.

VERSATILE STYLE Filling a small room with a lot of furniture will just make the space look cluttered and uninviting, no matter how much you love each item. It is useful to look at each object and see if it can be used in different ways. For example, I have an old desk chair in the attic that I use while writing at my desk, and it also serves as a little table on which I can rest a stack of books and perhaps a cup of tea beside my soft chair in the corner.

A LIGHT IN THE WINDOW Twinkle lights add a feeling of mystery and magic in the confines of a small room. Instead of hanging them up around the room, I have corralled a string of lights into an old tin candleholder in the shape of a house. They emit a softly diffused glow, which is especially charming on a cold winter's evening.

BEHIND THE CURTAIN The janitor at the local school, where I taught for some years, once presented me with a set of old pigeonhole shelves that the school no longer needed. As luck would have it, they were the perfect size to house magazines. I made a little curtain across the front to add charm to this rather tired-looking piece of furniture. For a similar effect, you could use some wooden planks and clean bricks to build up a pigeonhole design against a wall, then add a curtain in front (see page 49). With a little ingenuity, you will have created a perfect receptacle for your magazines.

PORTRAIT GALLERY Personal treasures within such a room bring back treasured memories and inspire feelings of contentment. In my attic room, various family photographs line one wall. The frames are all different, but they have all been painted in the same color to unify the collection.

WICKER WORKS Baskets of every shape and size are not only beautiful to look at but are extremely useful. They provide storage for a host of objects from tealights to pillows. I always want those who visit me to feel comfortable, so extra pillows and coverlets are always close at hand, stored in the many baskets that decorate my home. They make a corner look inviting and they are very simple to move about when redecorating. In this room, I have an old laundry basket that contains a selection of welcoming quilts and pillows. This size is ideal in a small room to keep it from looking cluttered.

SMALL WONDERS Finding and collecting small treasures is very addictive, but displaying these finds can be difficult due to their size and shapes. My father understood this delight in all things miniature, and helped me find the perfect solution. For Christmas many years ago, he surprised me with a little table that he had made from an old wooden printer's tray with lots of small compartments, to which he had added legs and a glass top. Here I store my absolute favorite bits and pieces, which bring back fond memories. The glass protects them from dust and dirt and the table is a useful spot for my tea tray.

COVER TO COVER You may think that wallpapering a small room with many angles will make the room feel smaller and too busy. On the contrary, papering every little nook and cranny will transform an ordinary space into something unique and special. As long as you paint all the baseboards/skirting boards the same color and keep window treatments simple, the room will become a sanctuary of calm and tranquillity. For wallpapers similar to this floral design, there are a few brands I would recommend: Sanderson, Colefax and Fowler and Cabbages & Roses.

"A wonderfully old-fashioned atmosphere pervades this little room and encourages daydreaming."

Make ideas

Painted Glazed Cupboard with Gingham Curtain

I was very excited when my friend offered me this sweet glazed cupboard, which had once housed her parents' collection of china figurines. I could picture it painted a soft white, with a red gingham curtain inside the glazed door. Old furniture made from deep, dark wood can be lovely in its natural state; however, I looked at the cupboard carefully and eventually decided that its brown shiny exterior was not the look I wanted. I decided to paint it, but I left the inside intact.

MATERIALS

old cupboard with glazed doors • masking tape • sandpaper • cloth • paint – I used School House White by Farrow & Ball • paintbrush • ruler • fabric scissors • red gingham cotton fabric • needle and thread • curtain wire • 2 sets of hooks and eyes

1 Place masking tape along the edges of the glass.

2 Lightly sand the entire cupboard, then wipe it down, making sure it is clean.

3 Lightly paint the cupboard and let it dry, then repeat for the second coat.

4 If you want a worn look, sand the areas that would naturally receive wear and tear from everyday use, such as the edges of the cupboard and around the handle.

5 Cut the fabric 1½ times the width of your glazed area and 3¼in/8cm longer than the height of the cupboard. Hem on all sides so that the frayed edges are hidden.

6 Fold the top and bottom of the hemmed fabric so that it fits the glazed area exactly. Making sure that you have left room to insert the curtain wire, sew along the edge to create a channel for the wire.

7 Insert the wire at the top and bottom of the curtain, making sure that the wire is approximately ½in/1-2cm short of the eyes.

8 Add eyes to the ends of both pieces of wire.

9 Inside the cupboard door, attach hooks at the four corners of the glazed area.

10 Hang up the curtain and admire your handiwork.

Armchair Mends

In a room that is created just for yourself, it is not essential to have robustly upholstered furniture. I have covered many old chairs with vintage pieces of fabric that have seen years of hard work, so wear and tear is inevitable. Mending these items is an enjoyable task and the same techniques work for clothing, too. The saying "make do and mend" is so apt for cozy living.

MATERIALS

fabric scraps • needle and thread • fabric scissors

1 Take a piece of fabric slightly larger than the hole you wish to cover.

2 Fold the raw edges underneath and simply whip stitch the fabric onto the material of the chair. It is up to you whether you allow the stitches to be seen or try to make them disappear.

3 Snip off the excess threads for a neat finish.

PART **2**

THE COZY OUTSIDE

CHAPTER 10

LINGER:
the porch

Porches grace many houses in my hometown in rural Canada. In the hot summers, a shady porch is a welcome retreat, from which you can easily strike up a chat with neighbors and passers-by. When I was living in London, a porch was unattainable, but when we moved to Buckinghamshire, my ideal porch became a reality. It is a wonderful canvas to decorate for the seasons. Collecting elements from nature is a most joyful and fulfilling task. A basket of pinecones by the porch door, fresh flowers on a rustic table and a wreath on the door will add warmth and style to your home.

Last Christmas, I met some gardeners felling branches from a tree and asked if I could take some home. When I got to the porch, I put the branches in buckets and threaded twinkle lights all around. I left the branches there until spring, replenishing the buckets with fresh water from time to time. Imagine my surprise when, one sunny morning, I was greeted by a miniature forest of flowering willow branches. Welcoming nature into your home is fundamental to a simple and natural life.

A porch offers huge scope for the imagination. I found some old Lloyd Loom chairs at a local summer fair. I added some homemade pillows and a quilt or two. On chilly evenings, woollen sweaters and some spice-scented candles will let you linger late into the night. One year I hosted a cozy Hallowe'en, with witches' hats seemingly floating with the help of invisible thread.

A porch offers a first glimpse of your domain, its cozy exterior leading visitors into your home. If you don't have a covered porch, many of the following ideas can be applied to a front door instead. A little attention to detail, something to say "welcome in", is all you need.

OUTDOOR DISPLAY An outside space is an extension of your indoor rooms, so why not make room to display your collections? I have a small shelf that holds buckets with flowers, jars with candles or and lovely old tins. On the hooks below I may hang up an apron or a quilt. It is an ever-changing vignette that just needs imagination to bring it to life.

CHALK TALK I was a school teacher and librarian for many years, and the joy of a chalkboard never diminishes. The squeak of the chalk is so familiar, and it allows me to write a seasonal message at any time. The board on my porch has an old French candleholder on each side of the board to create some ambience.

MAGIC LANTERNS We all enjoy the sight of a candle in the window at any time of the year. Hanging lanterns from the porch ceiling is a quick route to instant coziness. Just make sure that they are shielded from the elements, and extinguish the candles before you head indoors. When using jam jars as lanterns (see page 157), always make the hanging loops from wire, as string can burn. I also hang some lanterns from the trees in my garden so that they can be seen from the porch.

LEFT The old Swedish bench on my porch is used for more than just seating. At various times it may hold baskets and buckets of flowers, heaps of quilts or a copious amount of throw pillows. It should summon to all who see it to please come and sit for a spell. The porch is covered, so items placed on the porch will remain dry. Gathering fresh blooms for buckets to sit upon the porch is ideal as the blossoms remain fresh so much longer outside.

Porch style ideas

BENEATH YOUR FEET

I usually have a plain braided rug, one of several from my collection, adorning my front porch. They are made from leftover fabric scraps and are very easy to wash. My favourite is the one I received from my friends Chris and Kathy, who live in New York. It is a very old example of "make do and mend". This rug has seen many years already and I will make sure it sees plenty more. Its history and integrity give it a charm that a brand new doormat with hard coir bristles could never match.

In the winter, I cut fresh evergreen branches to use in place of a mat. The needles act like the perfect scraper and the warm fragrance is a bonus. When the branches start to look too worn to be of any use, I simply place them on the compost heap.

SEATING AND STORAGE

Having a bench that seats three comfortably is ideal in a small area. Add plenty of throw pillows and quilts and everyone will be very cozy. Storage can be a problem if you love to change your porch around. I added two old wooden apple crates that fit perfectly under my bench. They look good and are extremely useful when I need to store extra blankets or lanterns.

BENDING THE RULES Creating a wreath can be as easy as bending a twig into a circle, or as elaborate as you want (see page 142). A circlet of wire with a fabric heart tied to it is all you need for Valentine's Day. Try reusing an old wreath base and adding fresh flowers or greenery. Simply look at what nature has to offer and use your imagination – there are no rules, only ideas.

FAVORITE FRAMES I look out for chippy painted wood in any colour, as I know my husband will be able to make something from it. I love to place seasonal pictures in my porch – magazine pages, postcards and even wrapping paper become works of art when framed by him. Anything that is not too small will work well here.

LET THERE BE LIGHTS Outdoor lighting has an enchanting allure. I made sure that I had an electrical outlet installed on my porch for just this purpose. If you are creating a new porch, it is easy to install an outdoor outlet opposite an existing one inside your house.

A TOUCH OF TIMELESSNESS Adding corbels and shiplap to your porch not only adds beauty but makes it look as if it has always been there. I wanted my porch to have an old-world feeling, so I clad the ceiling in tongue and groove and chose simple supports for the roof. Everything is painted white, making it a blank canvas for natural, seasonal decorative elements.

AN OPEN DOOR A stable door is a wonderful finishing touch to this space. Leaving the top half of the door open connects you to the indoors, where a breeze gently drifting in from the porch will entice others to come out for a moment's relaxation. If the top half is glazed, add simple fabric curtains and look out for trick-or-treaters on Hallowe'en night.

NOSTALGIC CHARM Although hardly a new idea, bunting never goes out of style (see page 142). Little triangles of scrap fabric hanging from some string or wire always bring a smile to my face. I make bunting from old pillowcases, sheets, worn-out shirts – I even made some ribbons and different types of string from my collection. All it takes is a little time and a festive feeling will prevail.

Make ideas

Twig Garland

I really love using the variety of materials that nature provides. Twigs or vines can provide an abundance of creative ideas from nature's floor. It is extremely satisfying, not to mention free. This make is particularly apt for the autumn.

MATERIALS
twigs • wire • garden snips/secateurs • twinkle lights (optional) • fresh or dried hydrangea blooms • leaves

1 Put two twigs together and attach them together with wire, bending them to create a circle. Keep adding twigs until you have a wreath you like.

2 Alternatively, to make a straight garland, hang up a long piece of wire, then attach twigs securely along it.

3 Once all the twigs are in place, thread through the twinkle lights, if using.

4 Add hydrangeas and leaves to finish your garland.

Simple Bunting

Bunting conjures up happy thoughts of parties and celebrations. It is not necessary to have perfect triangles, nor do they need to be the same size. Uneven and imperfect wedges give the bunting a natural and carefree look. For this bunting, very little sewing is needed. Search your linen cupboard for old pillowcases and sheets if your fabric bag is empty!

MATERIALS
fabric scraps • fabric scissors • needle and thread • string • safety pin

1 Cut as many triangles as you need for your bunting – you will need an even number.

2 Take two triangles and put them together, right sides facing inward. Sew the top of the triangles together, but do not sew down the sides.

3 Turn right side out and sew another seam about ¾in/2cm below the first seam, creating a channel for the string to pass through. Take care not to make it too wide – you want the triangles to sit tightly on the string.

4 Repeat steps 2 and 3 for the remaining triangles. I think it is particularly pretty to use two different fabrics per triangle pair.

5 Once you have all your triangles finished, attach the safety pin to the string that will hold all the triangles. Thread them all onto the string.

6 Hang up the bunting and see how the triangles flutter in the breeze. When you wash them, the edges of the fabric will fray, adding more texture to the decoration.

CHAPTER 11

ENTERTAIN: the outdoor room

As the weather begins to cheer up after a long winter, our thoughts turn to the outside world. Homes that have porches, terraces or decks can easily extend their living area to the outside. We have been spending more time at home these past two years and this has encouraged many of us to find new ways to enjoy our outdoor spaces. What better idea is there than finding an underused area in your garden to turn into a private sanctuary?

In my garden, I have created more than one area in which to linger longer. My porch is my favorite spot, allowing me to enjoy the outside whatever the weather. Should this not be a possibility in your home, try to design something using what you already have.

Perhaps you have an old shed in your garden. Most sheds are only used to house the lawnmower and garden tools, but they often have great potential. Imagine tidying up this space so that the tools have their spot yet you can also carve out a place for yourself. Add a coat of paint, some fabric, a cozy chair and a little table and you will have already begun to create a new outdoor room. You could also add a pergola to the outside of the shed and train fragrant rambling roses and wisteria to climb up it.

Sheds are such amazing buildings to enhance. When we moved here, there was a rather sad-looking shed in the garden. It sat upon a long stretch of concrete, which we soon dug up to make a bigger lawn for our children to play on. The shed was moved into the corner of the garden. The only paint I had at the time was white masonry paint. I could not wait to transform the structure, so I quickly gave it a wash of this paint. It actually turned

ABOVE *Lovely lavender is a very welcome plant in my garden. Sprinkled throughout all of the beds, its fragrant blooms grow particularly well against the walls of my home. Lavender also attracts bees, which are essential pollinators. The old pine table holds my many flower-filled buckets that change to reflect the seasons.*

out to be the best idea. I am not sure how, but this paint created a distressed look that I love so much and it has lasted for more than 20 years.

We have made a few other changes to the shed over the years, mostly by reusing and upcycling materials that were headed for landfill. It received a new roof, thanks to a disused World War Two air-raid shelter. When a friend renovated their kitchen, the old flooring found a new life here. The workbench was our kitchen hutch/dresser, which we removed when we created a walk-through from the kitchen to the living room.

TOP ROW *An outdoor seating area tucked among the foliage creates a feeling of intimacy and coziness. Adding little jars of flowers to decorate your outside table is always a good idea. Add to that some mismatched pottery and you could not have a more inviting arrangement. Old farmhouse tables look exquisite covered with vintage lace tablecloths.*

BOTTOM ROW *The combination of red gingham pillows and a red, white and blue quilt says summer to me. A sign on my porch announces that this is the home of The Cozy Club – my crafting group, founded in 2008, where "you are a stranger only once". An iconic Adirondack chair looks fresh and inviting in all seasons.*

The quaint stable door was a dumpster/skip find. I added the gingham curtains, and planted lavender and roses in a haphazard fashion outside. The shed was, and still is, a delight. More recently, it has become my husband's retreat and "Crooked Workshop".

When the boys were little, I created a firepit in a corner of the garden so that we could roast sausages and marshmallows and pretend we were on a camping trip. Wanting to create a more permanent area, we added some gravel and delineated the space with bricks dug into the ground. I added a few old benches and wicker chairs, which I painted white, and some apple crates repurposed as side tables. Plants were added here and there – there was no plan, but I made sure to plant a few of my favorite lilac trees. These provide a delightful fragrance in the spring and make the area feel cozy and private due to their dense, heart-shaped leaves.

My front garden came about in a similarly unplanned way. Our Adirondack chairs are lovely, but they were too big for the seating area behind the house. We decided to move them to the front, where I had already made a gravel area. The chairs surround a smaller firepit made from our neighbor's old stove. The striking white of the chairs against the hedge and more lilac trees is perfect.

RIGHT *One can never have too many quilts, indoors or out. I cannot remember how many times I have said those words, especially when I am standing in front of a heap of them at a fair. Although I think they are priceless, I believe that the way to honor the maker is to keep using and caring for them with love.*

OPPOSITE *Candlelight plays an important role in my life. Its soft glow brings such warmth and cheerfulness to a room, and the porch is no exception. Lanterns dotted about on the porch throw out a welcome signal to all who see them.*

ABOVE *Placing a simple wreath upon a door is a lovely way to greet visitors. Having a hook fixed upon the door makes changing the decoration very easy. This heart-shaped hook was forged by hand in Nova Scotia. It is beautiful even without a wreath attached to it.*

This new area has now become another cozy outside room. I added some twinkle lights to the trees that surround the gravel area, which is a wonderful setting in the still summer evenings or frosty winter nights.

If you live in a city, a full-size outside room may be impossible. If you have a balcony, you can create a little oasis with plants and comfortable seating. For those who have no outside space at all, the only suggestion I have is to bring the outside in. Gathering twigs and winding twinkle lights through them will welcome friends and family into your living space. Herbs on a windowsill, fresh flowers and houseplants will provide color, scent and flavorful ingredients for cooking. Whether you have acres of land, a town garden, a balcony or nothing at all, if you live with nature and welcome it in at any opportunity, you are choosing to live a simple and cozy life.

ABOVE *For the benefit of winged insects and other creatures, I have allowed my grass to grow in a wild, but still orderly fashion. This untamed area is the perfect spot to place a chair for reading.*

LEFT *These white painted wicker chairs hark back to another time. Try to find inexpensive chairs, then paint them the color you would like and add some homespun pillows.*

Outdoor room style ideas

MENDING FENCES For as long as I can remember, I have loved picket fences. Perhaps this love was inspired by the many books that I read as a child. My dream was always to have a house framed by such a fence. They are so beautiful, but they require annual upkeep. A dirty and flaking picket fence just lets passers-by think that the house is in disrepair. However, driving home and seeing the welcoming white fence in the distance is worth every minute of painting and cleaning. I find the best time to repaint is at the end of winter, just before the leaves begin to unfurl. At this time of year, when the fence is more exposed, it is easier to apply the paint and you do not risk hurting any plants.

SEEDLING FAN I have yearned for a greenhouse for many years, but it was never a practical idea with the boys playing ball games within the confines of the garden. I have a path that leads into my back garden, which is not very wide and could never house a greenhouse. However, I knew it would be the perfect spot for a potting bench. I acquired an old, broken one with the knowledge that my husband could apply his woodworking magic to it. The bench now sits happily against a wall that was not being used at all. I painted it in the same color as the window frames and doors of the house. If you do not have a potting bench, a simple shelf supported by bricks against a wall will be perfectly sufficient to start off your seedlings.

WAITING FOR SPRING Planting up bulbs in the autumn is a joyful task. Imagining what will appear in the spring is a thrilling anticipation. All you need are some terracotta pots, potting soil and some grit for the base of the pot. I love to use Victorian pots that I find at fairs and flea markets. It does not matter in the least if they are chipped – it just adds to the charm. These also make wonderful presents for green-thumbed friends.

WATER STORAGE Water is a precious natural resource that deserves to be conserved carefully. Having containers in your garden to collect rainwater is one of the best things you can do for the environment. Adding a piece of charcoal to your containers will keep the water fresh.

AN IDYLL IN AN INSTANT A cluster of mismatched pillows and quilts is all that is needed to transform an ordinary corner in your garden into a welcoming oasis, but these will need to be kept indoors when not in use. Having a set of baskets to keep them in, as well as a designated area for storage, will make it far less arduous to set up your lovely space.

RAIN CHAIN Collecting rainwater to be used in the garden is a good use of our natural resources, but plastic downpipes are unsightly. I have replaced my downpipes with a humble metal chain, which is attached to the bottom of the gutter run-off. To install a chain, place three screws into the run-off pipe to form a triangle. Attach thick wire to each screw, which then will be attached to the top of the chain. When the rain comes, surface tension and gravity will do all the work for you.

A GOOD FIRE A firepit is wonderful in an outdoor garden room (see page 157). The key to building a glowing fire instead of a smoking heap of wood is using the right ingredients. First, gather up plenty of dried pinecones and small twigs. You can also add dried herbs for fragrance. Avoid using loose newsprint, as this will create smoke, and colored paper, which contains harmful chemicals. When the flame is burning brightly, slowly add bigger logs; these should be well seasoned and unpainted. Always remember that a small, carefully managed fire is preferable to a wild blaze that can rapidly get out of control.

ON THE LINE As anyone can attest who has donned a fresh garment that has dried on the line in the sun, the accompanying scent is gorgeous. Find a spot in your garden where a rope can be strung up on which you can dry your clothes. Seeing clothing, sheets and quilts swaying with the breeze is such a lovely and old-fashioned sight, and drying your laundry in this way is much better for the environment than using a dryer.

HOMEGROWN HERBS Anyone can enjoy the benefit of the taste of fresh herbs. Grown near a sunny window, they can provide you with organic delights for every meal. A lovely tea can be made simply by gathering a handful of fresh mint and pouring boiling water over it. Let it steep for a few minutes before drinking and the delicious tingle of mint will stimulate all your senses. If you have a lot of herbs in your garden and winter is approaching, consider snipping them into an ice-cube tray and freezing them. You will be rewarded with that delightful summer fragrance and delicious flavor whenever you want it.

IN FULL BLOOM There is something very rewarding about harvesting your own bounty of fresh flowers. The best way to do this is to collect them in the early morning and place them into warm water as soon as possible. Recut the stems diagonally if they have been out of the water for a while. Do not let any leaves stay submerged in the water. Make sure you renew the water on a daily basis and move the flowers into a cool area at night if you can. They will reward you by lasting much longer.

"If you live with nature and welcome it in at any opportunity, you are choosing a simple and cozy life."

Make ideas

Simple Firepit

This garden feature has become a must-have. I have had my firepit for more than 20 years. The reason that I built it was that I wanted my boys to experience cookouts similar to those I enjoyed as a child in Canada. I wanted them to learn how to have a fire responsibly, give fire the respect it needs and, most importantly, enjoy a natural garden activity.

MATERIALS
spade • grill • about 20 bricks • dry twigs and pinecones (for kindling) • bucket of water

1 Use a spade to clear an area the size of the pit you want to make. Use your grill as a size guide.

2 Start placing bricks to make a circle, then add layers to build up your firepit. The holes between the bricks will let air in to help keep the fire going.

3 Check to make sure the grill fits the diameter of the pit and then you are ready to make a fire.

4 Keep your bucket of water near the fire as a safety precaution.

See page 154

Glass Jar Lantern

It is easy to make an outdoor room a magical place for you and your friends. Collect as many jars as possible and repurpose them as lanterns to transform an ordinary space into a dreamlike retreat.

MATERIALS
wire • pliers • glass jar • tealight

1 To work out how much wire you need, wrap the wire once around the circumference of the jar under the lip. Multiply this length by five and snip the wire.

2 Fold this long piece of wire in half and twist three times at the fold to make a loop.

3 Hold the loop of the wire against the jar, under the lip as before. Wrap the wire halfway around the jar and make another loop in the doubled wire, opposite the first loop.

4 Continue wrapping the wire around the jar and then twist it together with the first loop to secure it.

5 Bend the remainder of the wire up and over the jar to make a handle and secure it to the second loop on the other side.

6 Add a tealight and hang up your lantern in a tree, making sure the jar is not too close to any branches.

Lap Trays

Serving a meal outside in your garden is a joyous experience. However, if a table is not available, eating can become difficult. Using a simple board as a lap tray from which to eat is ideal. Once you have enough lap trays for everyone, eating together around a firepit will be a delight.

MATERIALS
plank of wood • ruler • pencil • saw • sandpaper • paint and paintbrush (optional)

1 Cut several boards 12 x 8in/30 x 20cm in size, one for each tray.

2 Smooth the cut sides with sandpaper.

3 Paint the surface of the trays if desired.

CHAPTER 12

TEND:
the garden

I remember being given chores to do in the garden when I was very young and still living with my parents. Tasks included mowing the lawn once a week, sweeping the deck and weeding. At the time, none of these jobs received a lot of enthusiasm, but there was always a feeling of satisfaction when the work was complete. Now anything to do with the garden, even the most mundane task, is greeted with a lot of excitement. I love nothing more than spending a day in my patch of the earth. Seeing things flourish is the best antidote for any ailment.

In our first home, my husband and I lived in a garden flat. The outdoor space was filled with weeds and not much else when we moved in. Slowly I began to add a few flowers. I created a little path out of a heap of old cobblestones left over from a neighbor's renovation. Little by little, the small garden grew and, with it, my desire to spend more and more time looking after it. I read books and magazines, but my best teacher was my mother, who had passed onto me all her thoughts and experiences as a gardener when I was a child. Although I did not know it, I had stored all of her hints and recommendations in my mind and now, as I work, her voice is in my head helping me along.

Gardening can be a pleasure whether you have a balcony, a backyard or 100 acres. The process is the same. It is the love of nature, the joy of growing and the

willingness to look after the land that makes you a gardener.

I have learned so much tending my garden here in Buckinghamshire for the past 20 years, and it has gone though many transformations. When we arrived, much of the plot was covered with cement. I had no initial plan or design – it all just happened as the various plants and trees came along. When my boys were younger, the garden was mainly a playground. I did fence off an area where I could grow vegetables and flowers safe from cricket bats and footballs.

Within the past 10 years the garden has become my domain, and flowers and trees have taken over. I have made cozy areas in which to sit and dream, to cook and to catch the last of the sun's rays on summer evenings. Many of my plants came to me as presents from friends and family, so I am reminded of loved ones every day as I watch them grow and thrive.

ABOVE *Take a good look at your windows. Is there room to add a shelf for potted plants? Unlike a window box, a shelf allows for a quick and easy change without the need for planting.*

ABOVE *Tucked among the long grasses and under a tall cherry tree sits one of many old farmhouse tables from my collection. This long table gets carried out from the house when I am hosting a gathering, to be decorated with lanterns and buckets of flowers. Chairs will be dotted about for easy access. The dappled shade from the*

tree makes this a comfortable place to sit in hot weather – it feels like a fairytale setting.

RIGHT *A large wreath is a great way to add some colour to an outdoor festivity. A few fresh flowers add charm to a rustic homemade garland (see page 142) – there is no need to cover the whole base.*

I let nature do her thing and have never used pesticides. The occasional time that I have an infestation, I make a mixture of soap and water and spritz the bugs. The amazing thing is that when you live alongside nature, nature gives you a helping hand. Just by letting the grass grow, I have encouraged many different species of birds and insects to visit my garden and feast upon the bugs that are not welcome.

Creating your own sanctuary does not have to mean spending vast amounts of money. You can simply cover a patch of ground with a permeable layer and then add pebbles to make a nature-friendly seating area. Think about a spot in your garden that faces your house. To me there is nothing nicer that walking down a path to an unexpected location to sit back, look upon your home and enjoy the fruits of your labor. Seating can be as simple as an old tree stump or a few chairs brought out from your kitchen. Looking for proper garden furniture can be difficult, but I tend toward collecting old benches and chairs that have seen many gardens in their time, and then I enjoy repairing them. Painting inexpensive wicker chairs with outdoor-friendly paints

OPPOSITE TOP ROW
A white-painted arch with roses and clematis winding through it is a welcome sight at the front of a house. An old maple syrup sap bucket on the gate is planted with a gorgeous campanula. Hydrangeas are plants that just keep on giving. In the early summer they produce masses of blousy blooms in jewel-like tones and by late summer, they begin to turn deeper shades of green and rose. These can be dried to preserve them.

OPPOSITE BOTTOM ROW
Rhododendrons have evergreen foliage that creates a perfect hedge, and in the spring, huge blooms appear in stunning colors around the children's playhouse. Plenty of roses have found their forever home in my garden – I have bought all of them from David Austin's specialist nursery as bare-root specimens. Lilacs are another favorite of mine. My most prolific tree was given to me by my parents when we moved here.

RIGHT *This shed was built using parts from an old, dilapidated building. The window is covered with a piece of a threadbare quilt. It is not difficult to create an oasis using lovely discarded items.*

ensures that they will last a few seasons, especially if you put them under cover for the winter. Add some lanterns or twinkle lights and your spot is ready to enjoy. I have recently created a new area in my front garden. Here I have placed my beloved Adirondack chairs, which remind me of home. They are repainted every year and are extremely comfortable. This spot has become a favorite, especially during this past year, as it allows friendly conversations with passers-by.

If you enjoy a barbecue, think about making an area safe from overhanging trees where you can create a simple fire pit. I made mine out of bricks (see page 157). This area has witnessed many wonderful celebrations as well as cozy romantic evenings. It is so much more preferable to cook here in the heat of summer than in a hot kitchen. It also adds an element of adventure. As darkness descends and the lanterns start to shimmer, the feeling of being on vacation somewhere exotic is intoxicating.

I keep one outside table in the back garden that is covered with plants and flowers in buckets. At the moment, daisies are on display, but each season has its turn: pumpkins in the autumn and spruce, ivy and rosehips in the winter. This setting is especially wonderful in the spring when we are all dreaming of warmer days after a long winter. It is filled with many different varieties of daffodils and just seeing their sunny faces is so uplifting. Your garden is an extension of your home – a spot where you can linger and a patch to cultivate as you see fit. Living with nature is the premise of a simpler, happier life. Allowing nature to guide us sustains us and our world. By respecting and nurturing it, you are living the natural cozy way.

Garden style ideas

ALL THE YEAR ROUND

Wreaths have got to be one of my favorite items with which to decorate. I have them hanging on my doors and walls both inside and outside my home. Just a simple circlet of rosemary hanging upon a nail gives me immense pleasure (see page 171). More often than not, my front door is decorated with a wreath that reflects the season. There are several means of making wreaths and the natural world provides ample ingredients. For instance, I have a grapevine growing at the side of my garden. Each year it is trimmed, and I use the excess vine to fashion wreaths. In the autumn there are many pliable vines that can serve as a wreath base. Making small wreaths from the bounty of your garden to give as presents or to decorate your home is indeed a special touch.

HERBAL HARVEST
A herb garden near your kitchen door is sure to delight with its exhilarating scents and delicious flavors. In a small garden, an old box or a disused sink will do perfectly as long as it has sufficient drainage. I will often head out to my garden to collect a few sprigs of mint to decorate my bathroom. The warmth of the room during a shower or a bath releases its energizing fragrance.

A LEANING LADDER
Old wooden ladders are far more beautiful than their aluminum counterparts. If you have one that is no longer safe for climbing, consider using it to brighten up a dark corner of your garden. I have mine leaning up against a large cherry tree. Here I hang lanterns and and small buckets of flowers. It is a whimsical spot where I like to stop and dream.

SPRUCE UP YOUR SHED Outdoor sheds have recently had an enormous resurgence in popularity. Once seen as just a place to store garden tools, they are now more of a feature and can play an important part of making your garden special. Painting a shed with matt black paint is at first rather daunting, but the results are worth it. I did this with my little Wendy house and play area. Not only do they look magical, the color enhances all the flowers and bushes that grow nearby. The structures seem to melt into the background, letting the plants take center stage.

Meanwhile, the old shed that houses my husband's workshop received a quick coat of white paint. It is surrounded by a matching white picket fence. I planted roses and clematis around the shed so that now it supports these climbers. It has become a romantic area of my garden, even though it serves a useful purpose.

Fixing up an ordinary garden shed only requires imagination. If there is room inside, place a small bench covered with a mattress, quilt and comfortable cushion. This provides a shady spot to relax and read and all your gardening implements can be stored neatly to one side. In the off season, the shed can store all your summer furniture. Flowers in buckets and pots add immeasurable charm and a coat or two of paint can transform this place into something extraordinary.

LET IT GROW This is the first year that I have not cut my grass during the summer months. I have always had an area that I left uncut to help the birds and bees, but never the whole lawn. I absolutely love it. Not only is there less work, the garden has become a haven for wildlife. Gardening experts have extolled the virtues of "no mow May" and "too soon June". Daisies and buttercups grow happily alongside the tall grasses. I really enjoy the natural effect. A small path mown around the beds is very pretty and allows you to see what is growing in the garden. Making paths that lead here and there creates a mysterious and charming landscape.

CRYSTAL CLEAR If you like to have a little sparkle surprise you now and then, try hanging some glass crystals from the trees in your garden. Old crystals often have little holes in them so that it is easy to string invisible thread through the hole. Hang them where they will catch the light and look out for the shimmer.

EVERGREEN SCENE Christmas is a time for Christmas trees and I like to have small live ones dotted about my home during the season. I keep them in buckets and pots so that they grow at a slower rate. After the celebrations are over, I return these little trees to the outdoors. They are grouped together to form a little forest. Here they are tended and loved until the Yuletide returns. As long as they are watered and not kept in the warmth for too long, they will reward you with years of pleasure.

GROWING OLD GRACEFULLY Often, when antique hunting, you may come across an old chair or bench that looks as though it will not survive another day. Instead of passing it by, consider if you may have a place in your garden where it could weather away naturally. I have tucked an old bench among my rhododendron bushes. It is not for sitting on, but you can just see the bench and it looks like a scene from *The Secret Garden*. Old buckets and watering cans add to this illusion and those who come to visit you will no doubt be enchanted if they happen upon such a scene.

UNDER THE ARBOR

Arches create intrigue and delight in a garden. Consider placing an arbour in areas other than the typical entrance way. I love my arbor that welcomes people into my front garden, but I also have arbors of ivy and rambling roses in hidden spots within my garden. One leads to my compost heap, another to a wood store. They are very appealing and give the garden so much interest.

OUT FOR LUNCH Gather some blankets and a basket of food and head out into the garden or a local park for an impromptu picnic. If a garden is not available, there is nothing stopping you from heading to a park. Pack a wicker basket with a blanket and some simple sandwiches and you are off on an adventure. Use real plates and glass bottles (with stoppers) filled with homemade cordial. Linger over your lunch and take joy in your surroundings. I have no doubt that you will feel renewed and revived by enjoying some time outdoors.

TABLE TALK I cannot have enough tables in my garden. From small Victorian ironwork designs to old kitchen farmhouse tables, all find a spot to call home here. They each receive pots of plants or buckets of blooms to create a still life. Looking out into the garden from the house and seeing the various tables all strewn with flowers is a marvellous sight to behold.

Make ideas

Dried Flower Press

There is something quite beautiful that happens when you come across a dried flower pressed between two pages of a vintage book. Immediately you start to imagine the reason why this flower was saved. Perhaps the scent still lingers ever so slightly, and the fragrance transports you to a different time. Imagine making a book filled with such flowers to be tucked into letters or cards at a later date. Pressing flowers will enable you to keep the summer season with you even in the depths of winter. I used an old book, but any will do as long as you do not mind not being able to read it again.

MATERIALS
book • PVA glue • fabric scraps • brown parchment paper • fresh flowers for pressing • ribbon • heavy books to use as weights

1 Divide the pages in the book into small sections (for example 10 pages) and glue all the pages in each section together.

2 Let these pages dry completely.

3 Cut the fabric scraps into small patchwork pieces and start to glue them onto the book cover in a pleasing pattern. Cover the entire book to your heart's content.

4 Using the parchment paper, place the fresh blooms you want to press between the thick pages of the book. Close the book and tie a pretty ribbon around it to hold in the flowers.

5 Place the book under some heavier books. Your flowers will be dry and ready to use in about a week, depending on the thickness of the petals.

Dried Rose Petals

Having your own selection of dried rose petals to hand is just lovely. Whether strewn upon a table for a special dinner party or simply left in a jar to remind you of lazy summer days, these preserved petals will evoke wonderful memories. For my wedding, my aunt dried petals from her roses to use as confetti. I still have a handful of those petals to remind me of that special day. The best time to collect the flowers is in the early morning before the oil has evaporated.

MATERIALS
fresh rose petals • wire cooling rack • clean glass jars

1 Heat the oven to a very low temperature. Lay the petals on the cooling rack in a single layer.

2 Place the rack in the oven for 20-30 minutes, checking occasionally. Do not let the petals go brown. They are ready when they are slight crispy to the touch yet retain their color.

3 Let the petals cool completely, then store them in clear clean glass jars.

Rosemary Wreath

Homespun wreaths say "welcome" so beautifully. They are easy to make and a joy to hang throughout your home. Here my focus is on how to make a simple rosemary wreath, but do try various plants and see what you can create. As long as the stem can withstand being bent, it will make a wreath. You can also add little straw flowers or different herbs. The wreath will dry out after a few days indoors, but will still look nice. If left outside, it will remain fresh for much longer.

MATERIALS
rosemary • garden snips/secateurs • thin floristry wire • ribbon or string

1 Cut several sprigs of rosemary, the longer the better.

2 Put two pieces of rosemary together and attach them together with wire, bending the stems to create a circle.

3 Keep adding sprigs until you have a wreath you like.

4 Tie the ribbon or string to the top of the wreath and hang it up indoors or out.

Herb-infused Oils and Vinegars

These would make thoughtful presents from your garden to friends and family. Saving them to give at Christmas would be especially joyful, as they taste of summer. Feel free to try out different flavors, such as garlic and peppercorns or lemon peel and mint.

MATERIALS
herbs of your choice • heatproof bowl • pot • olive oil or vinegar (I like to use apple cider vinegar) • strainer • clean glass jars

1 Place a good handful of your chosen herbs in the bowl, saving a few sprigs to use as a garnish. For an oil I suggest using thyme, basil, oregano or rosemary, and for vinegar try dill or sage.

2 In the pot, heat the oil or vinegar until almost boiling.

3 Pour the hot oil or vinegar over the herbs in the bowl and leave to cool.

4 Strain the mixture and discard the herbs, as they are no longer fresh and will not look very nice.

5 Pour the strained oil or vinegar into pretty glass jars, then add a fresh sprig of two of the herb that you used.

RESOURCES

THE COZY CLUB

thecozyclub.co.uk

IG: @thecozyclubx

I founded The Cozy Club in 2008. It is a place of cozy gatherings where you can make, create and meet kindred spirits. The General Store is a purveyor of all things homespun, along with a lovely selection of vintage items.

UK BROCANTE & ANTIQUE FAIRS

ARTHUR SWALLOW FAIRS

asfairs.com

IG: @asfairs

THE COUNTRY BROCANTE

thecountrybrocante.co.uk

IG: @thecountrybrocante

THE DORSET BROCANTE

thedorsetbrocante.co.uk

IG: @thedorsetbrocante

FABULOUS PLACES

fabulousplaces.co.uk

IG: @fabulousplaces

UK SHOPS, MAKERS & ANTIQUE DEALERS

CAROLINE ZOOB

carolinezoob.co.uk

IG: @thestitchersjournal

Caroline, who wrote the foreword to this book, sells exquisite original embroidery kits. She also runs workshops and produces The Stitcher's Journal, a quarterly magazine devoted to embroidery.

THE COTTAGE HEN

etsy.com/shop/thecottagehen

IG: @the_cottage_hen

Fabrics and sewing supplies are on offer from modern-day textile merchant Kate Iles.

CUCUMBER WOOD CANDLES

cucumberwoodcandles.com

IG: @cucumberwoodcandles

Ruth Martin's delicious candles are made with love from soy wax and essential oils.

FABULOUS VINTAGE FINDS

fabulousvintagefinds.co.uk

@fabulousvintagefinds

Jess Walton and Simon Webb sell glorious vintage wares online and at fairs.

FARROW & BALL

farrow-ball.com

IG: @farrowandball

This paint brand is well known for its richly pigmented colors and high-quality finishes.

FORGET ME NOT ORIGINALS

etsy.com/shop/forgetmenotbookshop

IG: @forget_me_not_originals

Emma Williams uses vintage floral fabrics to create unique handmade book bindings.

GOOSE HOME AND GARDEN

goosehomeandgarden.com

IG: goosehomeandgarden

Sarah Kingston curates a beautiful selection of timeworn treasures for your home.

THE HATCHERY FARM SHOP

thehatcheryfarmshop.co.uk

This Buckinghamshire shop and café sells organic ready meals along with locally made jams and chutneys. There are also refilling stations for cleaning products.

HOME & VINTAGE LIVING

homeandvintageliving.co.uk

IG: @homeandvintage

Jules Langley mixes "the old with the new and a touch of the unusual".

HOOF BROCANTE

hoofbrocante.com

IG: @hoof.antiques_brocante

Kent-based Tara Franklin and Adrian Higham have a fabulous selection of antique textiles and furniture.

HUNTER GATHERER GIFTS

The Dairy House

Hanford

Blandford Forum

Dorset DT11 8HH

T: +44 (0)1258 861885

huntergatherergifts.co.uk

IG: @ huntergathereruk

Harriet Campbell's shop is a beautiful source of fun and unusual decorative items.

JUSTIN CRITCHLEY FLOWERS

T: +44 (0)7727 651741

justincritchleyflowers.co.uk

IG: @justincritchleyflowers

Based in Buckinghamshire, Justin sells gorgeous blooms collected with love.

THE KING AND I

tkandishop.com

IG: @thekingandishop

Clare Priestley's interiors, garden and lifestyle shop in Sussex is a magical place.

LITTLE WREN VINTAGE

IG: @littlewrenvintage

Emma Hood has a delightful collection of antique textiles and decorative items, which she sells online and at various brocantes and fairs throughout the year.

ROSABLUE

etsy.com/shop/rosablueoriginals

IG: @rosablue

Penny Menato makes enchanting dolls and clothing.

SUSSEX MEADOW

sussexmeadow.co.uk

IG: @sussex.meadow

Based on a farm in Sussex, Sophie Green offers a flower subscription service for her homegrown bouquets. Her two eco-friendly shepherd's huts are available to rent.

SUZI CHOPPING

IG: @suzihearts

Suzi creates special hand-stitched heirlooms from vintage quilts and fabrics.

CANADA

GIRLITURE DECOR
girliture.ca
IG: @girliture
Tanya Owen's shop in Kentville, Nova Scotia is full of pre-loved treasures lovingly restored and waiting for a new home.

SPRIG APOTHECARY
sprigapothecary.ca
IG: @sprigapothecary
Dea Sagnella is a purveyor of beautiful, natural products and fresh flowers in Mahone Bay, Nova Scotia.

WAYNE AND PAT McKAIG
IG: @bayfield_ca
Wayne and Pat's gorgeous selection of antique textiles and furniture can be found in the Southworks Antique Mall and St. Jacobs Antique Market, both in southern Ontario.

WILLOW COTTAGE QUILT CO
willowcottagequiltco.com
IG: @willowcottagequiltco
Alberta-based Andrea Flebbe runs this gorgeous online fabric store.

DENMARK

LIVSSTIL PÅ EGHOLM SLOT
livsstilegholmslot.dk
@livsstilpaaegholmslot
Situated in the grounds of Egholm Castle, this shop run by Katinka Louise Larsen and Anja Bøtker is a stunning destination for all things antique and vintage.

VINTAGE HOUSE DK
IG: @vintagehousedk
Beautiful vintage pieces from all over Scandinavia and France are hand-picked by Lisbeth Paulsen.

INDEX

Page numbers in *italic* refer
to the illustrations

Acknowledgments

This book would not have become a reality without several kind and amazing people.

Shirlie Kemp, a lovely friend and inspiring photographer. Thank you for joining me on this adventure and making each shoot day filled with joy and laughter. Your images are simply stunning, and you perfectly understood all the feelings that I was trying to portray.

Cindy Richards, who believed in the book and made it happen. Having worked with Cindy on three books, I can say from the bottom of my heart that it has been a complete pleasure. Her personal interest and contact made decisions easy and quick. I am forever grateful for her vision and honesty. Thanks so much, Cindy.

Sophie Devlin, an editor extraordinaire. Always available to help and advise, listen and suggest. You have been such a delight to work with and I cannot tell you how much I appreciate your prompt answers to my many queries! I count myself very lucky to have had you by my side through this process. Thank you so very much.

Until you actually write a book, you never have any idea how much work goes on behind the scenes. Sally Powell and Toni Kay are two people who create unseen, yet without them the book would not have reached fruition. They oversaw the layout of this creation and took to heart any ideas I had and interpreted them wonderfully. Thank you both.

To all at CICO Books, as I know there are many who have had an input, though I may never have met you. Your contributions have been invaluable, and I really appreciate all your work.

Caroline Zoob, an artist in every sense of the word. Her exquisite embroideries decorate homes around the world and her inspiring kits and *The Stitcher's Journal* encourage stitchers of every level. I met Caroline at The Country Living Fair more than 20 years ago. Her kind-heartedness and her sincere love of what she creates made her an instant kindred spirit to me. You have honored me with your words. Thank you.

To all my kindred spirits, you know who you are! Your encouragement and excitement that you shared with me as the book progressed have been amazing and my appreciation and love for you are unending.

How could I not mention the many thousands of you out there from all over the world who have connected with me on a daily basis through Instagram and Facebook? Your comments on my ramblings and photographs have been a joy and blessing for me to read. You have encouraged me to follow my dream and I hope that you see this book as a collaboration inspired by our shared values through the years.

"Everyone can identify with a fragrant garden, with beauty of sunset, with the quiet of nature, with a warm and cozy cottage."
THOMAS KINKADE (1958-2012), American landscape artist